Hugh Archibald Clarke

A system of harmony

founded on key relationship, by means of which a thorough knowledge of the rules

that govern the combinations and successions of sounds may be easily acquired

with or without a teacher

Hugh Archibald Clarke

A system of harmony
founded on key relationship, by means of which a thorough knowledge of the rules that govern the combinations and successions of sounds may be easily acquired with or without a teacher

ISBN/EAN: 9783744737678

Printed in Europe, USA, Canada, Australia, Japan

Cover: Foto ©Andreas Hilbeck / pixelio.de

More available books at **www.hansebooks.com**

A SYSTEM
OF
HARMONY

FOUNDED ON KEY RELATIONSHIP

36

By means of which a thorough knowledge of the rules that govern the combinations and successions of sounds may be easily acquired

WITH OR WITHOUT A TEACHER

BY

H. A. CLARKE, Mus. Doc.

PROFESSOR OF MUSIC IN THE UNIVERSITY OF PENNSYLVANIA

Philadelphia
Theodore Presser
1712 Chestnut Str.

Copyright, 1898, by THEO. PRESSER

PREFACE.

This work is not meant to be a theory of harmony, but a simple practical system, by means of which a knowledge of the mass of facts that form the basis of the art of composition may be acquired. Theoretical questions are therefore carefully avoided, and the tempered scale is accepted as the foundation of modern music.

The principal assumption or hypothesis upon which the system is built is the following:

No scale is an independent entity, but is only the principal one in a group of six called the *related group*.

The other is the reference of all dissonant groups to two roots in each scale.

The related group is of course familiar to all musicians, but it has never been used as the basis of a system of teaching harmony, to any great extent. The derivation of dissonant groups from a few roots is also quite familiar now, yet some departures from the usual manner of treating them will be found in this work, *not* for *theoretical* reasons, but for the gain of greater simplicity.

The plan of teaching laid down in this work is entirely new in several respects, and is based on the following maxims:

Teach one thing at a time.

Arrange the subject matter in such way that each step is a natural outgrowth of the last.

Teach the pupil how to use his knowledge, instead of simply trying to follow out the rule. Another departure from the usual practice is the complete discarding of the figured bass, with the result that all merely mechanical rotework is eliminated, and the pupil writes the chords because he *knows* what they are.

Many of the rules usually found in text-books are omitted; many of them are modified. For the reason that the so-called rules of composition have all been arrived at empirically, they are in a great measure, and ought to be altogether, deductions from the practice of those best qualified to say what should or should not be; viz., the great composers. It is a common subject of complaint on the part of the student that such and such things are laid down in the text-books as rules that must not be broken, and when he turns to the work of some great composer he finds them totally disregarded. His complaint is generally met by the reply, "When you can write like so and so, you may break the rules also." A wiser reply would be, Whatever has been sanctioned by a great writer becomes the property of all, provided they can use it with taste and discretion.

We do not wish to be understood as recommending to the pupil the instant disregard of all rules, because no one can learn how to break them until he has learned thoroughly well how to use them.

It being the business of harmony to teach the combinations and succession of sounds, very little is said in this book about the movement of parts, that being the province of counterpoint, which may be defined as the art of making the best use of the materials placed at our disposal by harmony.

H. A. CLARKE, Mus. D.
Professor of Music, University of Penna.

January, 1898.

CONTENTS.

INTRODUCTION — PAGE V

CHAPTER I. — PAGE 1
 Intervals.

CHAPTER II. — PAGE 6
 Major Scale.

CHAPTER III. — PAGE 9
 Major Scale and Common Chord.

CHAPTER IV. — PAGE 13
 Positions of Common Chord and Succession of Common Chords with Roots at Bass.

CHAPTER V. — PAGE 16
 Sequences of Common Chords.

CHAPTER VI. — PAGE 22
 First Inversion of Common Chord.

CHAPTER VII. — PAGE 27
 Second Inversion of Common Chord.

CHAPTER VIII. — PAGE 30
 Harmonizing of Melodies with Common Chords and their Inversions.

CHAPTER IX. — PAGE 33
 The Minor Scale.

CHAPTER X. — PAGE 38
 The Group or Circle of Related Keys.

CHAPTER XI. — PAGE 43
 Chords of Parallel Minor, Lowered Supertonic,— and Chords in the Related Keys not Found in the Given Key.

CHAPTER XII. — PAGE 51
 Chord of Dominant Seventh,— First Progression.

CHAPTER XIII. — PAGE 56
 Chord of Dominant Seventh,— Second and Third Progressions and Succession.

CONTENTS.

CHAPTER XIV. — PAGE 60
Chord of Dominant Ninth.

CHAPTER XV. — PAGE 61
Chord of Dominant Eleventh.

CHAPTER XVI. — PAGE 72
Chord of Dominant Eleventh Continued,—Additional Remarks on Second Inversions.

CHAPTER XVII. — PAGE 76
Progression of Dissonant Chords by means of Related Sounds.

CHAPTER XVIII. — PAGE 83
Chord of Thirteenth.

CHAPTER XIX. — PAGE 87
Supertonic Harmony.

CHAPTER XX. — PAGE 91
Altered Chords,—Augmented Sixth,—Augmented Fifth,—Passing Seventh.

CHAPTER XXI. — PAGE 97
Suspensions.

CHAPTER XXII. — PAGE 99
Retardation.

CHAPTER XXIII. — PAGE 109
Changing Notes or Appoggiaturas.

CHAPTER XXIV. — PAGE 112
Passing Notes.

CHAPTER XXV. — PAGE 119
Minor Scale.

CHAPTER XXVI. — PAGE 123
Open or Vocal Harmony.

CHAPTER XXVII. — PAGE 126
Pedal or Organ Point.

CHAPTER XXVIII. — PAGE 130
Transition.

SUPPLEMENT. — PAGE 145
Tempered Scale,—Figured Bass.

INTRODUCTION.

Sound is produced by the motion of the air. This motion is communicated to it by the vibration of some material body. If the vibrations are irregular, the sound produced is called **Noise**; if they are regular, the sound produced is called **Musical**.

The means used for producing musical sounds for artistic purposes are:

1st. The vibration of a **Column** of **Air** enclosed in a tube, as in the flute and the flue-pipes of the organ.

2d. The combination of the column of air with a **Reed**, as in the clarinet, hautboy, and (in some degree) the human voice.

3d. The vibration of **Strings** set in motion by the fingers, or by a bow, or by hammers, as in the harp, violin, and piano. The brass instruments may be included among the reed instruments, as the lip of the player in this case performs the function of the reed.

4th. The vibration of the **free reed,** as in the harmonium.

Musical sounds are distinguished among themselves in various ways:

1st. As high or low (acute or grave), called **Pitch.**

2d. Loud and soft (forte and piano), called **Intensity.**

3d. **Quality** (timbre). By quality is meant that property of a musical sound by which we distinguish whether it is produced by a violin, or flute, or voice, etc.

4th. By the relative length of time the sounds last, called **Duration.**

Notation is a system of signs designed to represent the **Pitch, Duration,** and **Intensity** of sounds.

The signs used to designate **Pitch** are the **Staff** and the **Clefs**; to designate **Duration,** the **Notes**;

To designate **Pitch** and **Duration** together, the **Position** of the **Notes** on the **Staff** and their **Form**.

The **Staff** consists of five parallel lines, on, between, and above or below which the notes are placed. When the staff is insufficient, additional lines called **Leger Lines** (generally but erroneously written ledger) are used, and the notes are written on, between, above, or below them.

The **Clefs**, three in number, are placed at the beginning of the staff; they determine the letter name of the *line* upon which they are placed.

1st. The treble or G clef, 𝄞, used now only on the second line.

2d. The C clef, 𝄡 or 𝄡, used on the first line, is called the **soprano** or descant clef; on the third line, called the **Alto Clef**; and on the fourth line, called the **Tenor Clef**. The use of this clef on the first line is gradually being discontinued.

3d. The **Bass** or F clef, 𝄢, used now only on the fourth line, was formerly used on the third line also, and then called the baritone clef.

The **Pitch** of the G indicated by 𝄞 is that of the sound given by an open pipe sixteen inches long; of the C indicated by 𝄡, that of one twenty-four inches long; of the F indicated by 𝄢, that of one thirty-six inches long.

In vocal music the use of the G clef for the tenor voice has become almost universal. When so used its **Pitch** must be understood as being an **octave lower**; viz., that of the sound produced by a pipe thirty-two inches long.

The **Forms** of notes indicate their relative duration; their **Positions** on the staff their letter names.

Eight forms of notes are used; the duration of each is half that of the one that precedes it. The first and last forms are less used than the others; they are named:

Breve, or double whole note.	Whole note.	Half note.	Quarter note.	Eighth note.	Sixteenth note.	Thirty-second note.	Sixty-fourth note.
‖𝅂‖	𝅝	𝅗𝅥	𝅘𝅥	𝅘𝅥𝅮	𝅘𝅥𝅯	𝅘𝅥𝅰	𝅘𝅥𝅱

When eighth, sixteenth, thirty-second, and sixty-fourth notes are used in groups they are joined, thus, ♫ ♫ ♫ ♫ in instrumental music, but not in vocal, unless they are all sung to the *same* syllable, when they must also be enclosed in a line called a slur;

thus:  When sung to *separate* syllables they must not

be joined; thus:

sup - pli - ca - tion

A dot placed after a note, thus, ○• increases its duration by one-half of itself, making it equal to three of the note that *follows* it in the table above, thus, ○• = ♩ ♩ ♩; a second dot increases the duration by one-half of the first dot, thus, ○•• = ♩•♩ ♩ ♩.

Each note has an equivalent sign for silence, called a **Rest**, thus:

Whole rest.	Half rest.	Quarter rests.	Eighth rest.	Sixteenth rest.	Thirty-second rest.	Sixty-fourth rest.

Dots modify the duration of rests in the same way as that of notes.

The essential rhythm of music is indicated by dividing it into portions of equal duration by lines drawn across the staff, called **Bars**. The enclosed spaces are called **Measures**, but in ordinary speech are also called bars.

To indicate the rhythmic content of the measure, signs called **Time Signatures** are placed after the clef; these are the following:

¢ C or 4/4 2/4, called simple common time.

3/2 3/4 3/8 3/16, called simple triple time.

6/4 6/8 12/4 12/8, called compound common time.

9/4 9/8 9/16, called compound triple time.

The *lower* figure indicates the note taken as the unit of the *beat* or *pulse*; the *upper* figure, the number of these units that each measure must contain.

The first two signs, ₵ and ₵, are survivals of the old sign for what was called imperfect time; viz., a broken circle, which signified two beats in the measure. The first of these signs, ₵, always means two beats in the measure, and is called alla breve time; the ₵ without the line is the same as $\frac{4}{4}$; i. e., four beats in the measure.

The first four are called **Simple Common Time.** Common time means an even number of beats in a measure; *simple* means that a single rhythmic unit is contained in each measure. (₵ or $\frac{4}{4}$ is, strictly speaking, a compound of two rhythmic units, but custom includes it among the simple times.)

The second four are called **Simple Triple Time** because each measure contains three beats, or one rhythmic unit of 1, 2, 3.

The **Compound Times** are all made from **Simple Triple Time.** If the upper figure is 6, it signifies that two measures of simple triple are made into one; if the upper figure is 12, four measures of simple triple are made into one. Then, as 6 and 12 are *even* numbers, it is called **Compound Common Time.**

The last four consist of three measures of triple time made into one; and as the upper figure is the odd number 9, it is called **Compound Triple Time.**

A **Scale** is a succession of sounds ascending or descending from a given sound. There are two kinds of scale, **Diatonic** and **Chromatic.** A **Diatonic Scale** moves through the *letters* without omission or repetition. A **Chromatic Scale** *repeats* the letters, changing their pitch by means of signs called sharp (♯), flat (♭), natural (♮), double sharp (×), double flat (♭♭).

The interval between a given letter and the next above or below is called a *whole* tone if another sound comes between them, and a half tone if no sound comes between them. Natural half-tones are found between *E* and *F*, and *B* and *C;* in every other case, if a half-tone is desired between two letters, one or the other must be modified in pitch by means of a sharp or flat.

The sharp raises the pitch of a letter; the flat lowers the pitch of a letter. Therefore, to make a half-tone between *F* and *G*, the *F* must be *raised* or the *G* must be *lowered*, thus:

There are two forms of the **Diatonic Scale**. First, called the **Major Scale**, has the sounds so arranged that there is a half-tone between the third and fourth, and seventh and eighth. If the letter *C* is chosen as the starting note of a scale (called the **Keynote**), we get a scale of this kind without having to use a sharp or flat; therefore the scale of *C* is called the **Natural Major Scale**.

If we take the sounds of the scale of *C* and rearrange them, beginning with *A* as a keynote, we get the other form of diatonic scale called the **Natural Minor Scale**.

The *chief* difference between a major and minor scale is, that in the major there are two whole-tones from the keynote to the third letter; in the *minor*, a tone-and-a-half from the keynote to the third letter.

As the scale of *A* minor is a rearrangement of the sounds of the scale of *C* major, it is called the **Relative Minor** of *C*.

If a scale is begun on any other letter as a keynote, it is necessary to use sharps or flats to make the whole and half-tones fall in the proper places. When a piece of music is written in any of these scales, the sharps or flats that the scale requires are put at the beginning, and are called the **Signature**. Sharps and flats to the number of six may be used in a signature. These signatures are here given:

KEYS WITH SHARP SIGNATURES.

1. Key of *G*, or of its relative minor, *E* minor.
2. Key of *D*, or of its relative minor, *B* minor.
3. Key of *A*, or of its relative minor, *F♯* minor.
4. Key of *E*, or of its relative minor, *C♯* minor.
5. Key of *B*, or of its relative minor, *G♯* minor.
6. Key of *F♯*, or of its relative minor, *D♯* minor.

INTRODUCTION.

Keys with Flat Signatures.

1. Key of *F*, or of its relative minor, *D* minor.
2. Key of *B♭*, or of its relative minor, *G* minor.
3. Key of *E♭*, or of its relative minor, *C* minor.
4. Key of *A♭*, or of its relative minor, *F* minor.
5. Key of *D♭*, or of its relative minor, *B♭* minor.
6. Key of *G♭*, or of its relative minor, *E♭* minor.

Observe that the sharps always begin with *F♯*, and that they are always written in the order in which they are here set down. So also with the flats, which always begin with *B♭*; also, that *F♯* and *G♭* are identical in pitch.

If the number of flats be increased to seven, the keynote would be *C♭*, this being the same as *B*, which has five sharps. It is preferable to write in *B*, it being easier to read in the key which has the fewer modified letters. Keys with more than six sharps or flats often occur in the course of a piece of music, but the sharps and flats are then placed before the letters to which they belong.

When any sharp or flat, not found in the signature, occurs in the course of a piece of music, it is called an **Accidental.**

Accidentals affect all the letters on the *same degree* on which they are written, but their influence never extends beyond the measure in which they occur, except when they occur at the end of a measure and the same letter is repeated at the beginning of the next measure. (This rule is very generally disregarded now, and the accidental is repeated.)

The **Natural** is never used in the signature, except when in the course of a piece a change of signature occurs, when the old signature is canceled, thus: When the natural occurs in the course of a piece to cancel one of the sharps or flats in the signature, it is an *accidental*. But when it occurs for the purpose of *restoring* an altered note to its place in the scale, it is *not* an accidental.

The natural cancels the double sharp and double flat also. Therefore, if the double sharped letter is to be restored to its original place, the natural and sharp are combined, thus, ♮♯; if the letter is double flat, thus, ♮♭. The following illustration gives examples of all the subjects treated so far.

In piano music two staves are used, joined with a sign called a **Brace.** Immediately after the brace the **Clefs** are placed; then the **Signature,** then the **Time Signature.** In the second measure the natural is an accidental. A quarter and a half-rest are also found in this measure. After the fourth measure the signature is changed — also the time signature. Whenever either one of these is changed a **Double Bar** must precede the change.

The clefs and signature must be put at the beginning of every line, but *not* the time signature. Observe that in every measure the united duration of the notes and rests equals the rhythmic unit indicated by the *Time* signature.

In the eighth measure a whole-measure rest is indicated in the lower part. A whole-rest is always used for this purpose, without regard to what the time signature may be.

INTRODUCTION.

The duration of a note may be varied in another way; viz., by tying it to another or to several more on the same degree. This sign ⌢ is called a tie. The tie must be repeated for each note when several are tied, thus:

If the first note is marked with an accidental, it is not necessary to repeat it as long as the tie lasts.

The duration of a note is also indefinitely extended by means of a sign called a pause or fermata ⌢. The pitch of the G clef is often raised an octave by writing *8va*.................. over it. The octave higher lasts until the dotted line ceases.

The pitch of the F clef may be lowered an octave by writing under it *8vb*................... *8va* is an abbreviation of *ottava alta* (octave higher); *8vb* is an abbreviation of *ottava bassa* (octave lower).

The **Rate** of **Movement**, called **Tempo**, is indicated by Italian words, as, allegro, andante, etc.;

The **Intensity**, by *p*, *pp*, *ppp*, which stand for piano (soft), piu piano (softer), pianissimo (softest), *f*, *ff*, *fff*, which stand for forte (loud), piu forte (louder), fortissimo (loudest); sudden access of intensity, by >, or ∧, or *fz*; gradual increase of intensity, ⟨; gradual decrease, ⟩. Many other words and signs are used, but they may all be found in the Dictionary of Musical Terms.

Rules for writing the chromatic scale in any given key: In ascending, raise all the letters except the third and seventh.

In descending, lower all the letters except the first, fifth, and fourth.

When any one of the *major* chords in the scale accompanies it, think of it as a *tonic* chord and write accordingly.

Write in the same way, if the accompanying chord is its *dominant*. The notes that must be changed in accordance with this rule are marked ×.

INTRODUCTION.

If the accompanying chord is one of the *minor tonics*, or its dominant, write as though in that key, as follows: in ascending, raise all but the second and fifth; descending, lower all but the first and fifth.

The advantages gained by this method of writing the chromatic scale are two.

1st. It reduces the accidentals to the smallest number possible.

2d. It does not introduce an accidental that may not be found in the dominant harmonies of the related group with one exception, viz., $A\sharp$; and even this is possible as the augmented fifth in the dominant of G, and as the third in the supertonic harmony of its relative minor, E.

DEFINITIONS.

Motion is *similar* when two parts or voices ascend or descend together; *oblique* when one part is stationary while the other moves; *contrary*, when the parts move in opposite directions.

A degree is from one letter to the next above or below, whether distant a whole-tone or half-tone. *Conjunct motion* is motion by degrees; disjunct motion is motion by leaps; diatonic motion is from one letter to the next; *chromatic motion* is from any letter to an altered form of the same letter; as, A–$A\flat$ or A–$A\sharp$.

Enharmonic change is the substitution of one letter for another without changing the pitch; as, $C\sharp$, $D\flat$.

HARMONY.

CHAPTER I.

INTERVALS.

Harmony treats of the combinations of sounds of different pitch, and the successions of these combinations.

The basis of modern music is a series of sounds, each one of which differs from the one lying next above or below by an interval called a half-tone, semitone, half-step, or minor second.

If the two contiguous sounds are expressed by the same letter, as $C, C\sharp. B, B\flat.$ it is called a **Chromatic** half-tone; if by different letters it is called a **Diatonic** half-tone.

When the *same* sound is represented by *different* letters, as $C\sharp, D\flat$, it is called an **Enharmonic** change.

The difference in pitch between two sounds is called an **Interval**.

The number of letters included decides the **name** of the interval, without regard to the number of whole or half-tones it may include. Thus, $C-D\sharp$ is called a second because it includes two letters, while $C-E\flat$, which sounds the same (in the modern scale), is called a third because it includes three letters.

The **names** of the intervals within the limits of the octave are: **Second, Third, Fourth, Fifth, Sixth, Seventh, Octave.**

But every interval may be written in several ways; as, $C-D\flat$, $C-D$, $C-D\sharp$. It is therefore necessary to distinguish between the different **kinds** of interval bearing the same name.

This is done by the use of the following terms, added to the **name** to denote the **kind**: **Minor**, or small; **Major**, or large; **Perfect, Diminished,** and **Augmented**.

Intervals are also classified as **Consonant** and **Dissonant**. A consonant interval is one that gives repose to the ear. A dissonant interval is one of which it is necessary that one or both the sounds must move in a certain way to satisfy the ear.

Consonant intervals are farther divided into **Perfect** and **Imperfect**.

A perfect consonance is one that cannot be altered without producing a dissonance. An imperfect consonance is one that is equally consonant, whether major or minor.

A diminished interval results from the contraction of a minor or perfect interval.

An augmented interval results from the expansion of a major or perfect interval.

All augmented and diminished intervals are dissonant.

The motion of the member or members of a dissonant interval is called their resolution.

If the dissonance is minor or major, only one member is compelled to move; if it is augmented or diminished, both members must move, towards each other if the interval is diminished, away from each other if it is augmented.

Although there are five kinds of interval, there are not five kinds of *every* interval. Thus of seconds there are three kinds, viz.:

C–D♭, one half-tone, called minor second.

C–D, two half-tones, called major second.

C–D♯, three half-tones, called augmented second.

It is quite possible to put a diminished second, or a doubly augmented second on *paper;* but as neither are to be found in any possible combination or succession, they are excluded as of no practical use.

The third also exists in three forms, viz.:

C♯–E♭, diminished, two half-tones.

C–E♭, minor, three half-tones.

C–E, major, four half-tones.

The fourth exists in three forms, viz.:

C♯–F, diminished, four half-tones.

C–F, perfect, five half-tones.

C–F♯, augmented, six half-tones.

The remaining intervals within the limits of the octave may be found by inverting the letters of those just given. It will at once be evident that any interval and its inversion must together make an octave, thus, $\overbrace{C \underbrace{\quad 2d.\quad\ \ \overbrace{D\quad\quad\ }^{7th.} C}_{8v.}}$; and since twelve half-tones make an octave, an interval and its inversion must make twelve half-tones. Therefore, to find the number of half-tones in the inversion of a given interval, it is necessary only to subtract the number in the interval from twelve, the number in the octave; thus, in the second $C-D$ there are two half-tones, therefore there must be ten in its inversion, $D-C$; and as the number of letters from D to C is seven, we also find that the inversion of a *second* produces a *seventh*. Then the inversion of a *third* must produce a *sixth*, and the inversion of a *fourth* must produce a *fifth*.

Then, as there are three *kinds* of each interval, three *kinds* of sevenths, sixths, and fifths must result from their inversion; and the *nearer* each other the sounds are in the smaller interval, the *farther* apart they must be in its inversion. Therefore the inversion of a given interval always produces one of the opposite kind, with one exception; viz., the inversion of a *perfect* interval produces a *perfect* one.

The foregoing explanations will make the following table of intervals clear. (See page 5.)

Intervals may also be divided into diatonic and chromatic. Diatonic are to be found in the major scale and in the natural minor scale; chromatic result from the introduction of sounds foreign to the scale.

QUESTIONS ON CHAPTER I.

What is the smallest interval in the scale?
What is the difference between a chromatic and a diatonic half-tone?
What is an enharmonic change?
What is an interval?
What determines the *name* of an interval?
Give the *names* of the intervals included within the limits of the octave.
What terms are used to distinguish between the different *kinds* of intervals with the same *name?*
How are intervals farther classified?
What is a consonant interval?
What is a dissonant interval?
What farther division is made of consonant intervals?
What is a perfect consonance?
What is an imperfect consonance?
How is a diminished interval produced?
How is an augmented interval produced?
What is the nature of all augmented and diminished intervals?

What is meant by the resolution of a dissonance?
In what kind of dissonances must one member resolve?
In what kind of dissonances must both members resolve?
When both members of the dissonance must resolve, in what case do they approach each other? In what case do they separate?
Are there five *kinds* of every interval?
How many kinds of seconds are there?
What is the smallest one called?
How many half-tones does it include?
How many half-tones in the major second?
How many half-tones in the augmented second?
How many kinds of thirds are there?
How many letters are included in a third?
What is the smallest third called?
How many half-tones does it include?
What is the difference between a diminished third and a major second?
How many kinds of fourths are there?
What is the smallest one called?
How many half-tones does it include?
How many half-tones in a perfect fourth?
How many half-tones in an augmented fourth?
What does inverting an interval mean?
What interval results from any given interval and its inversion taken together?
How many half-tones are there in an octave?
How many half-tones in an interval and its inversion?
Given an interval, how is the number of half-tones in its inversion found?
What is the *name* of the interval produced by inverting a second? A third? A fourth?
What *kind* of interval is produced by inverting one that is major? One that is minor? Perfect? Augmented? Diminished?

NOTES.

(1.) These questions must be asked over and over, and the various intervals must be written, until the whole chapter is understood and committed to memory.

(2.) The half-tone is used as a measure for the intervals, it being more convenient than it would be to use both whole and half-tones.

(3.) Whole-tone and half-tone are used in preference to the German whole-step and half-step, their meaning being perfectly clear ever since they were first used in English.

(4.) Dissonant intervals are by many writers called *discords*. A *dissonant* is *pleasant;* a discord is something that never should appear in music.

(5.) The perfect fourth and fifth are by some writers called major. The diminished fifth is also called imperfect. The augmented sixth is called *extreme*, or extreme sharp sixth. The names adopted in this work seem more logical and less likely to confuse the student.

TABLE OF INTERVALS.

HARMONY.

SECONDS.
Minor. Major. Augmented.

1 2 3
Half-tones.

THIRDS.
Diminished. Minor. Major.

2 3 4
Half-tones.

FOURTHS.
Diminished. Perfect. Augmented.

4 5 6
Half-tones.

SEVENTHS.
Major. Minor. Diminished.

11 10 9
Half-tones.

SIXTHS.
Augmented. Major. Minor.

10 9 8
Half-tones.

FIFTHS.
Augmented. Perfect. Diminished.

8 7 6
Half-tones.

The intervals on the lower staff are the inversions of those on the upper staff.

CHAPTER II.

THE MAJOR SCALE.

A **Scale** (from Latin, *scala* = a ladder) is a succession of sounds gradually rising in pitch from any given sound to its octave.

A **Chromatic** scale is one that ascends (or descends) by half-tones.

A **Diatonic** scale is one that ascends (or descends) by whole and half-tones.

Two kinds of diatonic scale are used in the modern musical system: 1st, called the **Major Scale**; 2d, called the **Minor Scale**. 1st, the **Major Scale**: in this succession a half-tone is found between the third and fourth, and seventh and eighth degrees; consequently, if the scale is divided into two groups each containing four sounds, it will be found that these two groups are alike in consisting of two successive whole-tones followed by a half-tone, and that these two groups are separated by a whole-tone, thus:

$$C, D, E, F \mid G, A, B, C.$$

These groups are called **Tetrachords** (from two Greek words meaning four strings).

A major scale may therefore be defined as being formed of two Tetrachords separated by a whole-tone.

As the Tetrachord *must* consist of a succession of two whole-tones followed by a half-tone, if it begins on any letter but C or G it is necessary to alter the pitch of one or more of the letters to make it conform to this succession. It is for this purpose that sharps, flats, double sharps, and double flats are used. For example, if it be desired to write a Tetrachord beginning on A, the succession of *letters* will be A, B, C, D; but as the interval between B and C is a half-tone, and that between C and D a whole-tone, it is necessary to move the C closer to the D; therefore it is written $A, B, C\sharp D$.

If a Tetrachord is to be written beginning on F, the letters will be

HARMONY. 7

F, G, A, B; but as B is a whole-tone above A its pitch must be lowered by making it flat; thus, F, G, A͡, B♭.

By examining the following series of sounds it will be found that the Tetrachord that makes the second half of the scale of C is also the first half of the scale of G, and the Tetrachord that makes the first half of the scale of C is also the second half of the scale of F.

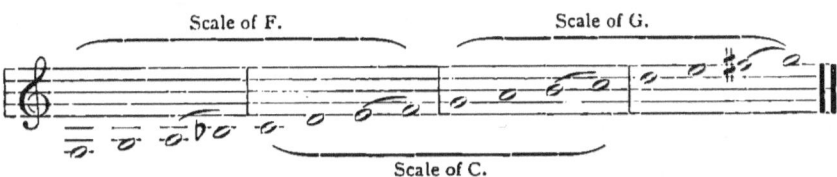

Therefore, **Every Tetrachord** belongs to **Two Scales,** that of the letter it **begins** with and that of the letter it **ends** with. These two scales are called **related scales.**

Therefore every major scale has two related major scales, one beginning on the *last* note of the *first* Tetrachord, the other on the *first* note of the *second* Tetrachord. (The easiest way to remember is, the *related major scales begin on the fourth and fifth of the given scale.*)

Every Tetrachord must contain *four successive* letters, and every scale must contain all seven letters and the octave of the letter it begins with.

It is this that necessitates the use of double sharps and double flats. Thus, if a Tetrachord is to begin on D♯, the letters will be D♯, E, F, G; but to make a Tetrachord they must be,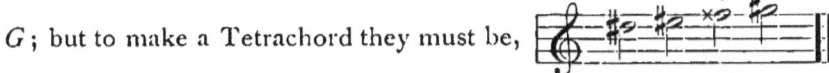

Or, if the Tetrachord begins on F♭, the letters will be F♭, G, A, B; but they must be written,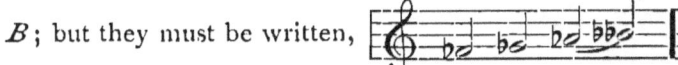

QUESTIONS ON CHAPTER II.

What is a scale?
What is a chromatic scale?
What is a diatonic scale?
How many kinds of diatonic scale are used?
Where do the half-tones occur in the major scale?
How may a major scale be divided?

Of what do these groups consist?
What are they called?
What definition may be given of a major scale?
Of what use are sharps, double sharps, flats, and double flats?
To how many scales does a Tetrachord belong?
What determines the scales to which it belongs?
What are these scales called?
How many major relations has a given major scale?
Upon which notes of the given scale do the related scales begin?
The pupil should write Tetrachords beginning with every sharp, flat, and natural, and should write over them the names of the scales to which they belong.

CHAPTER III.

Major Scale Continued, and Common Chord.

The following names are given to the degrees of the diatonic scale:
First, or keynote, is called the **Tonic**;
Second, **Supertonic** (upon or over the tonic);
Third, **Mediant**;
Fourth, **Subdominant**;
Fifth, **Dominant**;
Sixth, **Submediant**;
Seventh, **Leading Note**.

Mediant (from Latin *medius* = middle) is so called because it is half-way between the tonic and the fifth above, or dominant.

Subdominant (Latin *sub* = under) is so called because it is the same distance *below* the **Tonic** (a fifth) that the **Dominant** is above.

Dominant (Latin *dominans* = ruling) is so called because its harmonies rule or determine the scale. (Originally the dominant was so called in the ecclesiastical system because it was the principal reciting note of the chant.)

Submediant is so called because it is half-way between the tonic and the subdominant.

Leading Note is so called on account of its tendency to ascend to the keynote. (This note is also called the subtonic, in Latin *nota sensibilis*, in French *note sensible* = sensitive note, on account of this tendency.)

COMMON CHORD, OR PERFECT CHORD OR TRIAD.

A **Common Chord** consists of three sounds. The sound on which the chord is built is called the **Root**; the next is the **Third** above the root; the next is the **Fifth** above the root.

The third over the root may be major or minor: if major, the chord is called a **Major Chord**; if minor, the chord is called a **Minor Chord**.

The fifth over the root must be perfect; if it is not, the chord is not a common or perfect chord.

As there are only seven letters used in music, it follows that seven groups of letters must make all the common chords possible, as each letter may be the root, or the third, or the fifth of some chord, thus:

Fifths, E, F, G, A, B, C, D.
Thirds, C, D, E, F, G, A, B.
Roots, A, B, C, D, E, F, G.

It will be seen that to form a chord on any given letter, for example, A, it is only necessary to skip one letter to find the third, C, then skip another letter to find the fifth, E; thus, $A\ (B)\ C\ (D)\ E$. Therefore, there is an interval of a third between the root and third, and an interval of a third between the third and fifth. If from 1 to 3 is a major third, from 3 to 5 is a minor third; if from 1 to 3 is a minor third, from 3 to 5 is a major third; if from 1 to 3 and 3 to 5 are both minor thirds, the chord is called a **Diminished Chord** (or imperfect); if from 1 to 3 and 3 to 5 are both major thirds, the chord is called an **Augmented Chord** (neither are *common* chords).

In every major scale **Six** common chords may be written, (i. e. without using any accidentals). Three of these chords are major, three minor. The chords take the names of the degrees of the scale upon which they are written; therefore the chord on the

First is called the **Tonic Chord**, and is **Major**;
Second is called **Supertonic Chord**, and is **Minor**;
Third is called **Mediant Chord**, and is **Minor**;
Fourth is called **Subdominant Chord**, and is **Major**;
Fifth is called **Dominant Chord**, and is **Major**;
Sixth is called **Submediant Chord**, and is **Minor**.

The seventh or leading note may not be used as a root, because the fifth over it is diminished. (Diminished and augmented chords will be treated of in the proper place.)

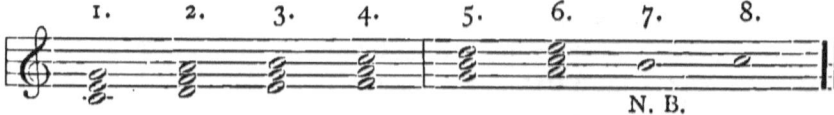

N. B. If B is taken as a root the perfect fifth is $F\sharp$, which does not exist in the scale of C.

It is important to remember that no change in the *order* in which the three letters forming a chord are written, changes the name of the chord. Thus the following example contains the chord of *A* only, because each group consists of the letters *A*, *C*, *E*.

Therefore, to find the root of a chord arrange the letters composing it to read (upwards) one, three, five.   (This rule should be borne in mind; it will be extended farther on.)

The pupil should be required to write major and minor chords, using every natural, sharp, and flat as roots. The following remarks will aid in remembering the perfect fifths.

I. Every fifth that may be struck on two *white* keys is perfect, except *B–F;* to make a perfect fifth between these letters, either B must be flat or F sharp.

II. Every fifth that may be struck on two *black* keys is perfect.

III. There are only two perfect fifths that have the root a white and the fifth a black key, viz., *B–F♯* and *C♭–G♭*; only two that have the root a black and the fifth a white key, viz., *B♭–F* and *A♯–E♯*.

Write the following chords in their natural positions, that is, root, third, fifth, and mark every chord major or minor, as the case may be.

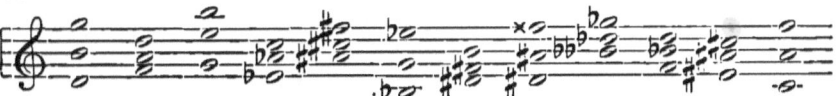

QUESTIONS ON CHAPTER III.

Give the names of the degrees of the diatonic scale.
What does supertonic mean? Mediant? Subdominant? Dominant? Submediant?
Why is the seventh degree called the leading note?
Of how many sounds does a common chord consist?
What is the sound on which the chord is built called?

What is the interval between the root and the next member of the chord? Between the root and the third member of the chord?
What *kind* of third may a chord have?
What is the chord called when the third is major? What when the third is minor?
What *kind* of fifth must a chord have?
How many groups of letters make all the common chords?
What is the interval between the third and fifth of a chord?
What *kind* of third is this in a major chord? In a minor chord?
If both these thirds are minor what is the chord called?
If both are major what is the chord called?
Are either of these common chords?
How many common chords may be written in a major scale?
How many are major? How many minor?
How are the chords named?
Give the names of the major chords.
Why may not the leading note be used as a root?
Does changing the order in which the letters of a chord are written change its name?
How may the root of a group of letters that form a chord be found?

NOTE. The teacher should insist that when pupils are giving the letters that form a chord, they must mention the sharps or flats *always*.

CHAPTER IV.

Position and Succession of Common Chords.

The lowest note of any group sounded together is the **Bass**. (This word should be spelled *base*, because the proper meaning of *bass* is a deep sound.)

It is not at all necessary that the bass note of a group be written on the "bass" staff.

Avoid any confusing of **Bass** with **Root**. The root may be the bass, but the bass may be any member of the chord. The first step in learning to use chords is to learn how to write successions in which the **Roots** are always the **Bass Notes**.

The most effective harmony is that written in four parts (or for four "voices"). Since the common chord has only three letters in it, it is necessary to repeat one of the letters to make a fourth part. When the root is used as a bass, the root itself is the best member to repeat; thus, C, E, G, C. It will be evident that while retaining the root C as a bass, it is possible to make three different arrangements of the remaining letters. Thus, instead of having the repeated root at the top, the third, *E*, might be, or the fifth, *G*, might be. Therefore we have this rule:

Every chord with its **Root** at the **Bass**, and with the **Root** repeated, may be written in **Three Positions**.

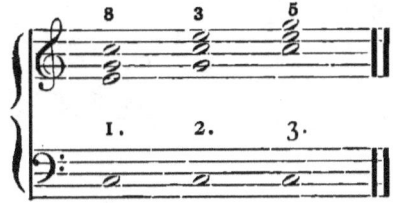

If the repeated root is at the top, it is called the **Octave Position** (1); if the third of the chord is at the top, it is called the **Tierce Position** (2); if the fifth is at the top, it is called the **Quint Position** (3).

For the present these positions are indicated by placing *over* the top of the group, 8 for octave, 3 for tierce, and 5 for quint position. (Pupils should be required to do this until they are quite familiar with the positions.)

It is necessary to remember that the term **Position** always means that the **Root** is at the bass. The first and most important rule to be observed when writing a succession of chords in **Positions** is — **Two Chords must never occur in Succession in the Same Position.**

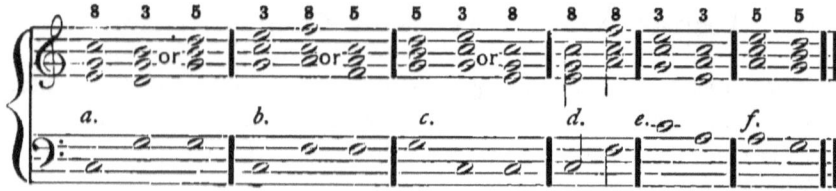

a. The first chord being in the octave position, the following chord may be in either the third or fifth position.

b. First chord, third position; the next may be octave or fifth.

c. First chord, fifth position; the next may be third or octave.

d. Both chords in octave position forbidden.

e. Both chords in third position forbidden.

f. Both chords in fifth position forbidden.

Consequently there is always a choice of two positions; viz., either of those in which the last chord is *not* written.

In general a better effect is produced when the three upper parts move in the opposite direction to the bass, especially when the bass moves only one degree. (More exact rules for this will be given later.)

The motion from first to second chord is called oblique — that means one part (the top) is *stationary*, the bass moves. 2 to 3 is contrary motion; the bass (*a*) moves one degree. 3 to 4 is direct or parallel motion; bass and top both ascend. At *b* the bass moves one degree.

HARMONY.

The following basses are to have the chords written over them in accordance with the foregoing rules. Do not be satisfied with simply getting the chords *right*, but try the effect of different positions.

These exercises should be transposed repeatedly and rewritten.

QUESTIONS ON CHAPTER IV.

What is a bass note? Must it be written on the bass staff?
How is four part harmony made from common chords? Which member is the best to repeat when the root is at the bass?
Do bass note and root mean the same thing?
What is meant by the position of a chord?
In how many positions may a chord with the root repeated be written?
What are they called and why? Which member of the chord is at the bass in all *positions?* Give the first rule for writing successions of chords in positions.
If a chord is in the octave position, what positions may the next chord have? What if it is in the third position? What if it is in the quint position?
What is meant by oblique motion? By direct or parallel motion? By contrary motion?
Which kind of motion is considered the best?
In what case is it especially to be observed?
Name the keys, the tonic, subdominant, and dominant chords, and leading notes of the exercises marked I. to VI.

CHAPTER V.

SEQUENCES OF COMMON CHORDS.

The movement of common chords is absolutely free; that is, any chord in the scale may be followed by any other one. Some of these successions will be found to be much smoother than others, but there is *no* succession that cannot be made to sound well when used in the right place. For example, the following passage  may be harmonized in the following ways:

1 is smooth but commonplace.
2 is more vigorous.
3 is rugged almost to harshness.
4 is dignified, with a savor of quaintness.

In 2 the progression from first to second chord, (i. e., from a major chord to the minor chord on the third above,) was not considered good at one time. In 3 the progression from first to second chord, (i. e., from a minor chord to another minor chord one degree above or below,) was forbidden. The progression from the second to the third chord, (i. e., from a minor chord to the major chord a third higher,) was not considered good.

No rule can be given as to when one of these harsh progressions will sound well and when it will not. The judgment of the composer as to the effect he wishes to produce is the only guide; but pupils should avoid this class of successions until they have thoroughly learned all those that are smooth and natural.

HARMONY.

There is one other progression that should be avoided; viz., from the subdominant to the dominant, except the subdominant is in the eighth and the dominant in the fifth or third position, thus:

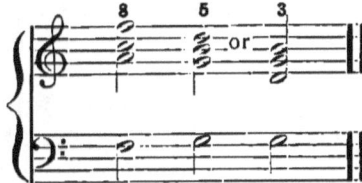

N. B. The above remarks must be understood as applying only to successions of chords in **Positions**; i. e., with their roots at the bass.

Common chords are frequently written in what are called **Sequences** (Latin *sequens* = following). In a sequence the roots move in a regular order or pattern, for example:  up four, down three. The result is three pairs of chords, each one degree higher than the last.

The most usual sequences are here given, both ascending and descending. The pupil should write them in various keys and should also exercise his ingenuity in constructing others.

a, b, c, are ascending sequences.
d, e, f, are descending sequences.

It is allowable to use the diminished (leading note) chord in a sequence for the sake of preserving the "pattern," thus:

The use of the diminished chord was sometimes "dodged" by the older writers in the following way:

The $B\flat$ is retained in the chord of G because $B\natural$ would necessitate a chromatic progression, $B\flat$, $B\natural$, which was forbidden in strict counterpoint.

Sequences composed of common chords natural to the scale are called **Diatonic** or **Contrapuntal**. They were much more largely used by the old school than by the new; still it is absolutely necessary that the pupil should familiarize himself with them. The reason why will appear farther on.

The **Positions** of the chords may be changed in all these examples; thus, Example *a*, page 17, may be *five, three*, or *three, eight*, or *three, five*, or *eight, three*, alternately, thus:

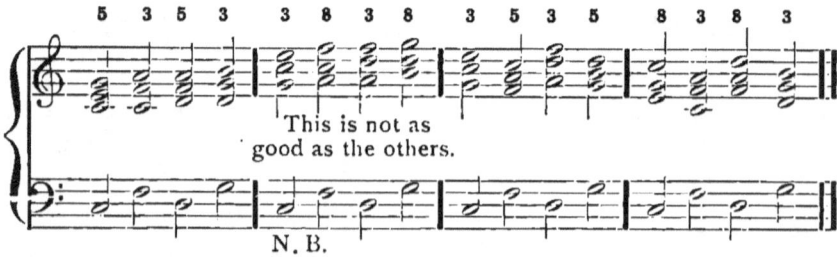

Observe that the best effect is produced when the outer parts move in opposite directions.

It does not sound well to move to a chord in the Octave Position with the Bass and upper part (soprano) moving in the same direction, except in the following cases:

I. From **Dominant** to **Tonic Chord**.

II. From **Tonic** to **Subdominant** chord. (The relation between these chords is the same as that of the previous chords.)

Another rule is often given, viz., that the eighth may occur in Direct Motion when the upper part ascends a half-tone; but whenever this is the case, it *must* be either a progression from **Dominant** third position to **Tonic** octave, or **Tonic** third position to **Subdominant** octave.

N. B. It is owing to the infraction of this rule that this passage does not sound well. Another progression that does not sound well is that to a Chord in the Quint Position with the outer parts (bass and soprano) moving in the same direction, except in the following case:

From any chord to another, the roots of which chords are a fifth apart (ascending), or what is the same, a fourth apart (descending).

Tonic. Dominant.   Subdom- Tonic.
                   inant.

Two chords may be written in succession in the Tierce Position by doubling the third of one of them.

If the roots ascend, double the third of the Second chord.
If the roots descend, double the third of the First chord.

(What sequences may be made of chords in the third position?)

20   HARMONY.

Two chords *may* be written in succession in octaves, fifths, or thirds when the outer parts move in opposite directions.

The last example (3) is frequently used. 2 is the most unusual. 1 is common at the end of a piece.

EXERCISES.

The pupil should be required to point out all the sequences that may be found in these exercises, also the places where examples of all the progressions mentioned in this chapter may be used. For example, in the first exercise the first two measures form a sequence; the three chords marked x may all be in the third position.

I.

Avoid unnecessary skips from one chord to the next.

II.

III.

IV.

V.

VI.

HARMONY.

QUESTIONS ON CHAPTER V.

Is there any restriction on the movement of common chords?
Give the successions that are mentioned as lacking in smoothness.
What is a sequence?
Is the use of the diminished chord permitted in a sequence?
What are sequences composed of chords natural to the scale called?
Give the cases in which an octave position may be taken in direct motion between the outer parts.
Give the cases in which a fifth position may be taken in direct motion between the outer parts.
How may two chords be written in succession in the third position?
Which of the chords has the third doubled when the roots ascend?
Which when the roots descend?
State the cases when two chords may be written in succession in octave, fifth, and third.

Note. When writing exercises draw a slur ⌢ under all the roots that form the sequence, also under succession of chords in third position.

CHAPTER VI.

First Inversion of Common Chords.

If the preceding chapters have been thoroughly mastered, the pupil will know all that may be done with the Common Chords natural to the Scale, with their Roots as Bass notes; i. e., in **Positions**.

The next step is to Invert the chords. Inversion means using some other member of the chord as a bass.

If the **Third** of the chord is used as a bass, the Chord is said to be in its **First Inversion.**

The **First Inversion** of a Chord is subject to no restrictions; that is, any chord in the scale may be written with its third at the bass.

When the Third is used as a bass, the **Root** or **Fifth** may be repeated (to make the fourth part); it is immaterial which.

a. Chord *C*, *E*, *G*, with the third, *E*, at the bass, the root repeated.

b. Same, with the root repeated at *unison*. This is signified by doubling the note.

c. Same, with the fifth repeated.

d. Same, with fifth repeated at unison.

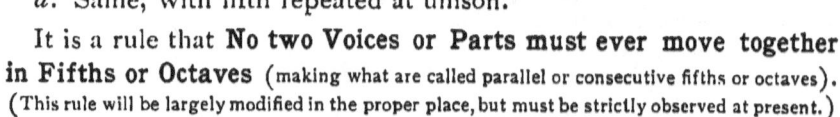

It is a rule that **No two Voices or Parts must ever move together in Fifths or Octaves** (making what are called parallel or consecutive fifths or octaves). (This rule will be largely modified in the proper place, but must be strictly observed at present.)

It is in consequence of this rule that it is forbidden to write two chords in succession in the same position.

a. Both in octave position; therefore the *first and fourth* parts move together in octaves, the *second and fourth* in fifths.

b. Both in third position; *second and fourth* in octaves, *third and fourth* in fifths.

c. Both in fifth position, *first and fourth* in fifths, *third and fourth* in octaves.

The doubling of the third, when two chords are written in succession in the tierce position, is sure to avoid the parallel fifths and octaves.

In writing the same Position twice in succession, the parallel fifths or octaves will always be found between the *bass* and one of the upper parts. If two First Inversions are written in succession, the parallel fifths and octaves will occur between two of the upper parts, thus:

a. Octaves between first and third parts, fifths between second and third, caused by repeating the root in both chords.

b. Octaves between first and third parts, fifths between first and second, caused by repeating the fifth in both chords.

Therefore they may be avoided by repeating the *Root* in one chord and the fifth in the other, or repeating one at unison, the other at the octave.

a. Both roots repeated— one at unison, the other at octave.

b. Fifth at unison, root at octave.

c. Root at octave, fifth at octave; but the repetition of the root makes an octave between the *first and third* parts, that of the fifth an octave between the *second and third* parts, and to be parallel, they must occur between the *same* two parts.

d. Both fifths repeated. The *first and second* parts being in unison, there is a fifth between them and the third part; but the second fifth is between the *first and second* parts.

e. The repeated *C* is root of one and fifth of the other chord; but these octaves are not *consecutive* because they are *stationary.* To be consecutive they must move.

f and g. Roots repeated, unison and octave.

Parallel fifths and octaves may also be avoided by repeating the Third of one or both of the inverted chords, provided the repetition of the Third is made by two parts moving in opposite directions.

The Third of a chord may be repeated at any time, if the repetition occurs in parts moving in opposite directions.

a. First and second chord inverted, the third of 2 repeated.

b. Second chord only inverted, its third repeated.

c. Third of second chord repeated.

d. Same.

e. The third of the same chord repeated. This case is peculiar as it really makes parallel octaves between the first and fourth parts, but they occur in opposite (contrary) motion. The long skip of the bass also helps to hide them.

f. The third repeated in both chords.

The above examples should be written in all the keys, until they are thoroughly understood and memorized. Then the exercises following should be written, care being taken to introduce examples of all the progressions here given.

Any bass note may be treated as a **Root,** or as a **Third.*** When it is treated as a third, put a 3 *under* it, and no figure *over* the upper part.

* *Note.* It is perhaps necessary to repeat that the leading note cannot be a root; therefore the second of the scale cannot be a third.

When a chord is **Inverted** it is *not* in any **Position**; therefore the chord that follows it may be in *any* position.

Analyze the following example, give the **Name, Position,** or **Inversion** of every chord. State which member is repeated, and give the *reason* of every repetition.

This example should be copied, and the chords numbered, and the analysis of each chord written out, thus:

1. Tonic chord, tierce position.
2. Supertonic, first inversion, third doubled by parts moving in opposite directions, and so on.

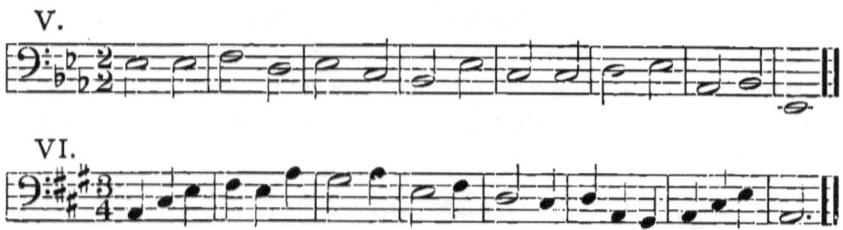

QUESTIONS ON CHAPTER VI.

What does the inversion of a chord mean?
Which member of the chord is at the bass in the first inversion?
Which chords in the scale may be used in the first inversion?
Which members of the chord may be repeated?
What is meant by parallel or consecutive fifths or octaves?
Between which parts will the parallel fifths or octaves be found, when two chords are written in the same position?
When two first inversions are written in succession, where will the parallel fifths or octaves be found?
How may these be avoided?
What is the rule in regard to the repetition of the third?
Which degree of the scale may not be a root? Which not a third?

CHAPTER VII.

SECOND INVERSION OF COMMON CHORDS.

When a chord is written with its **Fifth** as a bass note, it is called the **Second Inversion** of the Chord.

The use of **Second Inversions** is very much restricted.

A Chord in its **Second Inversion** is either a **Tonic**, a **Subdominant**, or a **Dominant**.

The **Second Inversion** of a **Tonic** may be used at any time, *provided* it is followed by the Dominant Chord. (Note the author is well aware of the rule which says, it must never enter with a leap in the bass, but fails to see the utility of rules that the greatest composers disregard.)

In **Second Inversions**, the fifth (bass note) is the best to repeat.

a. Second inversion of tonic, preceded by tonic. *b.* By supertonic. *c.* By mediant. *d.* By subdominant. *e.* By submediant. *f.* By first inversion of supertonic with third doubled. This succession and that at *d* are very smooth and *orthodox*.

Cadence (Latin *cado* = to fall). This term is applied to various kinds of endings. The Perfect or Authentic Cadence is the final tonic preceded by the dominant with its root at the bass. This is emphasized if the dominant is preceded by the second inversion of the tonic, and still more emphasized if the second inversion of the tonic is preceded by the subdominant (as at *d*) or supertonic (as at *f*).

EXAMPLES OF PERFECT CADENCE.

The **Second Inversion** of a **Subdominant** must be preceded by the **Tonic Chord** with its root at the bass. It is *generally* followed also by the **Tonic Chord** with its root at the bass.

The **Second Inversion** of the **Dominant** chord is preceded by the **Tonic Chord** with its root at the bass, and followed by the **Tonic Chord** with its third at the bass, or just the reverse. This second inversion is not often used on the accent of the measure. It is apt, in this case, to sound like a Tonic chord.

a and *b* are better than *c* and *d*, on account of the contrary motion between the outer parts.

Although the second inversions always *enter* as above, viz., if a tonic, after any chord in the scale; if a subdominant, after the tonic, root at bass; if a dominant, after the tonic, root or third at bass — they do not always conform to these examples as to the chord that follows them; but the rest of this subject must be reserved for a later chapter.

The exercises that follow are to be transposed to all the keys. They are the last basses that will be given.

QUESTIONS ON CHAPTER VII.

What is meant by the second inversion of a chord?
Which chords may be used in the second inversion?
What must precede the second inversion of a tonic?
What must follow it?
What must precede and follow the second inversion of a subdominant?
What must precede and follow the second inversion of a dominant?
What is meant by a perfect cadence?

CHAPTER VIII.

HARMONIZING OF MELODIES, WITH COMMON CHORDS AND THEIR INVERSIONS.

The knowledge of Common Chords now gained, must now be applied to the harmonizing of Melodies; first, with the Chords in Positions.

As every chord may be written in three positions, it follows that every note in a melody may be either the root, third, or fifth of some chord belonging to the scale. If it is treated as a root, the bass will be the same letter; if as a third, the bass will be the third letter below; if as a fifth, the bass will be the fifth letter below.

It is evident that if two notes in succession in the melody are treated as roots, or thirds, or fifths, the result will be two chords in the same Position.

Begin and end with the Tonic Chord. Observe that the melody may begin on the root, third, or fifth of the tonic. Be careful to avoid using the Leading note as a root.

The first time the exercises are written, observe carefully the rule, not to write two successive Positions alike.

The second time they are written, find as many opportunities as possible to put two or three successive chords in the Tierce Position.

Sequences are indicated in the Melody as they are in the bass, by the notes moving in a regular pattern. Thus, the following notes

 indicate the following Sequence:

 Others may readily be found by referring to the sequences in Chapter V.

HARMONY.

After harmonizing these exercises with chords in **Positions,** write them over again, introducing **First Inversions.** Then, for the last time introduce both **First** and **Second Inversions.** Analyze the following example of a melody, harmonized three times.

First time, chords in *position*.
Second time, first inversions introduced.
Third time, first and second inversions introduced.

Play these over, and observe how the musical effect improves with the use of the inversions.

Questions on Chapter VIII.

What member of a chord may any note in the melody be?
If treated as a root, what will the bass note be?
If as a third, how far below will the root be found? If as a fifth?
May two notes in succession be roots, or thirds, or fifths?
When may two or more notes be thirds?
What chord must begin and end the piece?

Note. A piece does not *always* begin with the tonic chord.

Must the first and final chord be in the octave position?

CHAPTER IX.

THE MINOR SCALE.

The Minor scale historically seems to have preceded the Major. Although its formation from two Tetrachords is not so evident as in the Major scale, yet it is nevertheless true. In the oldest form of Tetrachord the half-tone lay between the first and second letters; thus, E, F, G, A. A seven note scale (which preceded the octave scale) was formed by joining two of these Tetrachords; but the second Tetrachord began with the letter upon which the first Tetrachord ended; thus, E, F, G, A.

$A, B\flat, C, D$.

This was called the scale of Conjunct (joined) Tetrachords. It was made into an octave scale by adding a sound *below* the first Tetrachord; thus, D, E, F, G, A.

$A, B\flat, C, D$. This was known as the Dorian scale.

It will be seen that the half-tones lie between the *second* and *third*, and *fifth* and *sixth*. This form is now called the Natural Minor Scale.

It will be found that by taking the sounds of any Major scale and arranging them in an octave succession beginning with the sixth of the Major scale, it will give a succession identical with this; therefore,

Every Minor scale is called the **Relative Minor** of the major scale from which it is formed, and it has the same signature. (It is perhaps easier to remember the relative minor as beginning on the third *below* the tonic, this being the inversion of the sixth above.)

The requirements of harmony have made several modifications in this scale.

I. It is necessary to modern ears to have a half-tone between the seventh and eighth of a scale in ascending. If the seventh is raised, there results the awkward interval of an augmented second between 6 and 7; to remedy this, 6 must also be raised. But the need of a half-tone between 7 and 8 is not felt in a descending scale; they are therefore allowed to remain unaltered. This form of ascending and descending scale is called the **Melodic**, because the raised sixth and natural seventh are not found in any of the chords belonging to the scale. (See note.)

We have nothing to do at present with either of these forms, but with a third form called the **Harmonic**. In this the seventh is always raised, both ascending and descending. So the minor scale is always to be thought of at present as having a raised seventh or leading note. These three forms of minor scale are here given.

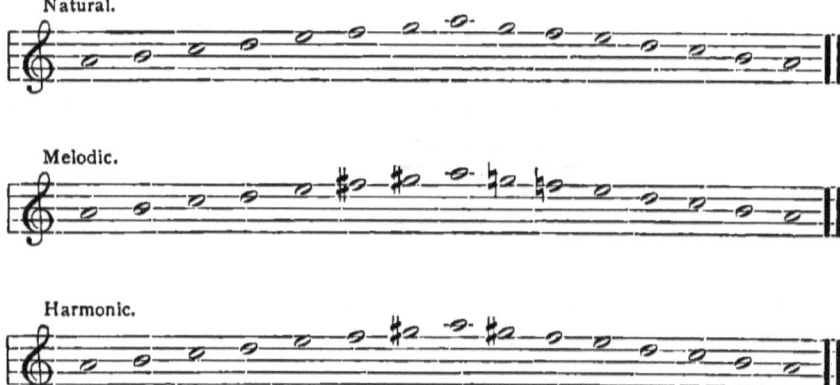

SCALE OF A-MINOR. THE RELATIVE MINOR OF C.

Natural.

Melodic.

Harmonic.

Four common chords may be written in the **Harmonic Minor** scale. Two are minor, viz., Tonic and Subdominant; two major, viz., the Dominant and Chord on sixth.

Dominant chords must be major. This is the harmonic reason for the raising of the seventh; hence this scale is called the **Harmonic**.

Note. In the older writers the raised sixth was harmonized as the fifth or third of a chord. It is rarely found in modern music. Another form of minor scale was also used by the older writers, called the mixed minor. In this scale the 6 and 7 were raised both ascending and descending. Consequently it differs from the major scale only in having the third above the tonic minor. This scale will be found frequently in Bach and Handel.

Scale of A-Minor, Harmonic, with Chords.

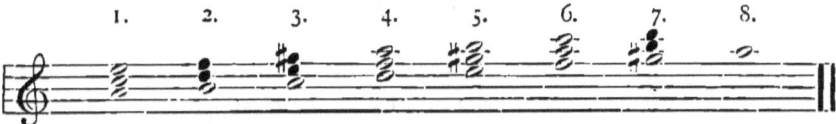

1. Tonic, minor.
2. The fifth is diminished.
3. The fifth is augmented, owing to the raising of the seventh.
4. Subdominant, minor.
5. Dominant, major. Observe that this is the only chord in the scale in which the *raised note* is found, and that it is the *third* in this chord.
6. Submediant, major.
7. Leading note, diminished fifth.

Analyze the following example:

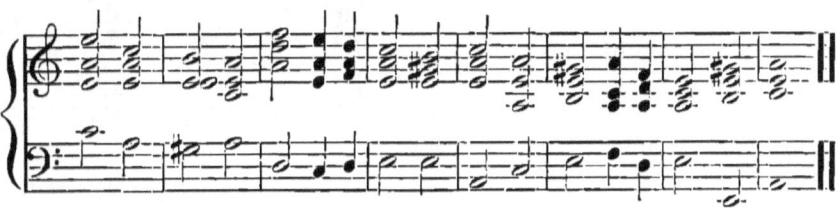

A **Major Scale** and its **Relative Minor** are so closely bound together that they may conveniently be looked upon as one and the same thing. Consequently if the seventh of the minor scale appears *not* raised, it is generally as a member of one of the chords in the related major scale.

2 is in the relative major.
3 and 4 in minor.
Part of 5 and 6 in major, the remainder in minor.

It was customary at one time to end all compositions in the minor key with a major tonic. This major third was called the "Tierce de Picardie." It is still occasionally used.

In harmonizing the exercises that follow, find opportunities for the use of the relative major chords. The *natural* seventh of the minor scale must (at present) be either root or fifth of a chord in the relative major.

It is necessary now to speak of the Diminished Chord, but more will be said about it later.

Diminished Chords may be used freely, with the proviso that they are used in the first inversion.

In the Major scale there is but one; viz., on the Leading note. In the Minor scale in addition to one on the Leading note there is one on the second (Supertonic) of the scale. This last mentioned chord is very important in the minor scale.

The Bass note of this chord is the best to repeat.

First inversion, bass repeated.

Diminished chord on second of *A* minor. (It will be seen that it is also the leading note chord of the relative major.) The second inversion of the tonic enters very effectively after this chord.

Questions on Chapter IX.

Where do the half-tones lie in the natural minor scale?
Why is a minor scale called the relative minor of a major scale?
Upon which degree of the major does the relative minor begin?
To what form of minor scale is the term *melodic* applied?
To what form is the term *harmonic* applied?
Where do the half-tones lie in the harmonic scale?
What is the interval between the sixth and seventh?
How many common chords are found in the harmonic scale?
Which are major? Which minor?
What kind of fifth does the *mediant* bear?
In which chord is the raised seventh found?
What member of this chord is it?
If the seventh is not raised, how is it generally treated?
Where are diminished chords found?
In what form may they be used?
Which member should be repeated?

CHAPTER X.

The Group or Circle of Related Keys.

In Chapter II. the relationship of Major scales through the Tetrachords is explained. In the last chapter the relation between a Major and its Relative minor is explained. This relationship must now be extended to include the Relative Minors of the Major Relations.

Thus, given the key of *C*, the related majors are *F*, *G*.

The relative minors *A*, *D*, *E*.

Thus a given key always includes a group of six keys, three Major keys and their Relative Minors.

Each of these scales must have a leading note; thus, *C* being the key, *F*, its first major relative has *E* as leading note. *G*, the second major relative, has *F♯* as leading note; *A* minor has *G♯*; *D* minor, *C♯*; E minor, *D♯*.

So *four* accidentals may be introduced in the scale of *C*, as leading notes to the related scales. We found that the leading note of the minor scale was only to be found in the dominant chord, in which chord it is the third. From these facts we deduce the following rule:

Notes *raised* by accidentals are Leading notes to Related Keys, and they are always harmonized as **Third** in the **Dominant Chord** of the key to which they lead.

The most natural progression of a Dominant chord is to its Tonic.

1. Dominant and tonic of *D* minor, relative minor of *E*.

2. Dominant and tonic of *E* minor, relative minor of *G*. (When there are two raised notes in a chord, the *last* one to occur is the third; therefore D♯, which does not occur until after F♯, is the third. *F* must be sharped in *E* minor because it is sharped in *G* major.)

3. Dominant and tonic, *F* major.
4. Dominant and tonic, *G* major.
5. Dominant and tonic, *A* minor, relative minor of *C*.
6. Dominant and tonic of Key.

It is much to be regretted that one word, modulation, is used to signify going into a related key transiently (especially by means of its dominant chord), and going *outside* of the related groups.

The writer has thought that for clearness' sake, the word *modulation* might be used only in the first sense, and that the word *transition* better describes this passing to a *new* group of relations. Therefore in this work these words will be used with this distinction between them.

In all the modulations in the foregoing example, the idea of the original key is never lost for a moment,—what is called the "Tonality." The reason, perhaps, is that the *Tonic chords* are simply the six common chords of the original scale. If one of these *Tonics*, when preceded by its dominant is changed, for example, if the tonic of *D* minor (1) is changed to *major*, the *tonality* of the original key is at once lost, and a *transition* is made.

The following examples will show how these dominant chords may be used.

a. Is harmonized with chords natural to the scale.
b. Same melody, with dominant chords of related scales introduced.

Harmonize the following passages in the same manner; follow every dominant by its own tonic for the present.

In 1 the dominant and tonic of *D* minor may be used.

In 2 the dominant and tonic of *A* minor and *G* major.

In 3 the dominant and tonic of *A* minor, *G* major, *F* major.

In 4 the dominant and tonic of *G* major, twice; or second place may have dominant *E* minor.

In 5 the dominant and tonic of *F, G, A.*

In 6 the dominant and tonic of *D, E.*

When these dominant chords of related keys are used in sequences, the sequence is called *harmonic* (or chromatic). Sequences will be found in *2, 3, 5, and 6* of the above examples. A few more are here given. They and the foregoing exercises should be transposed to every major key.

EXERCISES INTRODUCING RELATED KEYS.

The rules about second inversions may now be extended so as to include the Tonic, Dominant, and Subdominant chords of the Related keys.

1. Second inversion of some related tonics.
2. Second inversion of subdominants.
3. Second inversion of dominants.

Although the dominant chords *generally* progress to their tonics, they may — being *Common* chords — have other progressions, which may occur singly or be arranged in sequences.

1. Dominant, followed by the chord on the sixth of the scale to which it belongs.

2. Dominant of minor, followed by tonic of relative major. *a.* Both roots at bass. *b.* Tonic, with third at bass. *c.* Dominant, third at bass; tonic, fifth at bass.

3. Two dominants in succession. In this case the roots must be a fourth apart (ascending), or fifth apart (descending).

4. Dominant of a minor, followed by chord on minor third above.

5. Dominant changed chromatically to natural chord of scale.

6. Same as 4, but second chord with fifth at bass.

7. Dominant of a major key, followed by dominant of its relative minor.

1, 3, and 7 are of special importance.

Transpose these examples to all keys.

Questions on Chapter X.

How many scales are included in the related group?
How many are major? How many minor?
How many accidentally raised notes may be introduced in a given scale?
What are these accidentals?
What is the natural progression of a dominant chord?
What is the difference between a diatonic and a harmonic sequence?

CHAPTER XI.

Chords of Parallel Minor, Lowered Supertonic, and Chords in the Related Keys not Found in the Given Key.

In addition to the Dominant chords of the Related keys there still remain some Common chords which may be used without making a transition.

Taking *C* as our given key, the related key of *F* possesses two chords, *G, B♭, D* and *B♭, D, F*, that are not found in *C*. The related key of *G* possesses one that is not found in *C*,— *B, D, F♯*. See accompanying table of chords.

The use of these chords in the key of *C* is somewhat restricted, owing to the fact that they are not owned in common by the scale in which they are found and the given scale. Their use generally indicates a transition to one or the other of these related keys, which is continued for some time. The following examples are given of their use without a transition:

None of them, especially 3, sound quite at home.

The Major and Minor scales that begin on the same keynote are called **Parallel** scales. The chords belonging to a Minor scale may be used in its Parallel major. The Minor scale (harmonic) differs from its parallel major in two of its degrees only; viz., the third and sixth, which are minor, counting up from the keynote.

These sounds are found in three of the chords in the minor scale, thus:

One of them, the sixth, is also found in the Diminished chord on the Supertonic (which must be used, as already explained, in its first inversion), thus:

The Minor Tonic and Subdominant are often preceded by the major form of the same chord (1); or, the Minor Tonic by the Dominant (2); the Minor Subdominant by the Tonic (3), or by the Dominant (4).

The chord on the sixth of the Parallel minor may be preceded by the Tonic or Dominant.

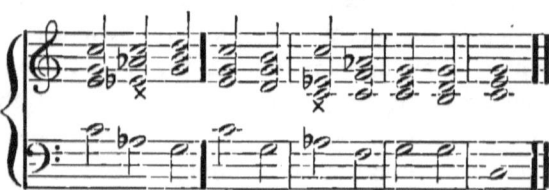

The chord on the sixth of the Major may be followed by the Minor Subdominant or Tonic.

The Minor Tonic may also be preceded by the Dominant of the Relative minor (1); and by the Dominant of the Relative minor of the first major relation (2).

The first inversion of the diminished chord on the supertonic is generally followed by second inversion of tonic; it may be preceded by any chord but the mediant.

The foregoing examples show what may follow as well as precede these Parallel Minor chords. The pupil should try the effect of all of these successions in different *positions* and *inversions* (in all the keys). It will be found that some progressions which sound well with one arrangement of the chords, are intolerable with another arrangement.

The last Common Chord is a Major chord on the **Lowered Supertonic** of the scale.

In the key of *C*, the **Lowered Supertonic** is $D\flat$; a Major chord on this root is, $D\flat$, F, $A\flat$. This chord, although used freely in the Major key, seems to sound more at home in the Minor key. If used in the Major key it may be preceded by the Tonic, Subdominant, Dominant or by any of the chords of the Parallel minor. It is followed by the Tonic or Dominant.

This chord is more frequently used in its first inversion (as in examples 4, 5, 6, 7) and is then called the **Neapolitan Sixth**.

In the example that follows, all the chords and progressions so far learned will be found. The analysis of it should be well studied. All analyses should be made on the following principles.

I. Every chord bears some relation to the principal key; that is, it is either to be found in that key or in one of its relations.

II. Every chord bears some relation to the Chord that precedes it.

III. Every chord bears some relation to the Chord that follows it.

IV. Every Major chord may bear five possible relations; viz., Tonic, Subdominant, Dominant, sixth of a Minor scale, Lowered Supertonic.

V. Every Minor chord may bear five possible relations; viz., Tonic, Subdominant, Supertonic, Mediant, Submediant. Thus, the Major chord C, E, G, in

1, bears the relation of Tonic to the preceding chord.

2, bears the relation of Dominant to the following chord.

3, bears the relation of Subdominant to the following chord.

4, bears the relation of Submediant to the following chord.

5, bears the relation of Lowered Supertonic (of B, followed by dominant).

The Minor chord A, C, E, in

1, bears the relation of Tonic to the preceding chord.

2, bears the relation of Subdominant to the following chord.
3, bears the relation of Supertonic to the following chord.
4, bears the relation of Mediant to the following chord.
5, bears the relation of Submediant to the preceding chord.

A Chord always bears a relation to the Chord that follows it differing from that it bears to the Chord that precedes it (unless the *same* chord precedes and follows).

This relationship may or may not make a modulation.

1. The chord A, C, E, enters as *Tonic*, and is followed by Subdominant chord, — all three in A minor.
2. A, C, E, enters as Tonic, but is Subdominant to the following chord, modulating to E minor.
3. Dominant of C, followed by chord on sixth of parallel minor. This chord, $A\flat$, C, $E\flat$, is then treated as the Lowered Supertonic of G, followed by Dominant of G.

Note. Common chords have been treated at great length and with especial fullness, because a thorough familiarity with them and their progressions is by far the most important part of harmony. The dissonant chords that follow will be found **easy** if the common chords have been thoroughly mastered.

1. Tonic. 2. Tonic parallel minor. 3 and 4. Dominant. 5. Submediant. 6. Supertonic. 7 and 8. Dominant *A* minor. 9 and 10. Tonic parallel minor. 11 and 12. Submediant parallel minor. 13. Lowered Supertonic followed by (14) dominant. 15. Tonic 16. Submediant is Subdominant to the next chord. 17. Tonic *E* minor. 18. Dominant *E* minor. 19. Tonic *E* minor. 20. Subdominant *E* minor, but mediant to the next chord (21) *F*, which is dominant to (22) *B♭*, which is lowered supertonic of *A*, followed by dominant (23) and (24) tonic *A*, treated as subdominant to *E*, 25. 26. Dominant of *E* minor, followed by chord with root a minor third above, 27. 28. Dominant of *D* minor, followed in the same way. 29. *C* minor, parallel minor. The two bars make

a sequence. 30. Dominant. 31 to 38. All belong to parallel minor, except 35, which belongs to both major and minor. 39 to 42. Are easily "parsed." 43. Subdominant of parallel minor, preceded by Submediant of major. 44. Tonic treated as sixth of *E* minor. The rest is easy.

It will be seen that the chords of the parallel minor may be written in succession.

EXERCISES INTRODUCING ALL POSSIBLE COMMON CHORDS WITHOUT GOING OUTSIDE OF THE GROUP OF RELATED KEYS.

QUESTIONS ON CHAPTER XI.

How many chords are common to the scales of C and F? Which are they?
How many to the scales of C and G? Which are they?
Are there any chords common to all three scales? Which are they?
What chords in F are not found in C?
What chords in G are not found in C?
What is meant by parallel scales?

In what respect does a minor scale differ from its parallel major?
In how many of the chords of the minor scale are these notes found?
Does the dominant of a **major** scale differ in any way from that of its parallel minor?
How is the minor tonic preceded? The minor subdominant? The chord on sixth?
What other chords may precede the minor tonic? The minor subdominant?
How is the diminished chord on supertonic of parallel minor generally used?
Is any other common chord possible? Where is its root? Is it major or minor? By what is it followed? By what may it be preceded? In what form is it most frequently used?
What name does it bear in this case?
How many relations may a major chord bear?
How many, a minor chord?

CHAPTER XII.

CHORD OF DOMINANT SEVENTH, FIRST PROGRESSION.

Dissonant chords are those that include a sound that must move in some specific direction. This motion is called the **Resolution** of the Dissonance. (The term *resolution* is rather loosely applied to the movement of *chords*. Chords *progress*, their Dissonant members *resolve*.)

All Dissonant chords are formed by additions to **Major Chords.** The most important are the additions to the Dominant chord.

Dissonances that are members of a chord are called *Essential* (to distinguish them from those that are merely ornamental, or that are used as Suspensions or Retardations).

The whole series of dissonances that may be sounded with a given root are called its **Harmonies.**

The first addition to the Dominant is the seventh over the root.

This seventh is minor; it resolves by *descending*.

Three Inversions may be made. The rules about second inversion of *common* chords do not apply to Dissonant chords.

The Dominant seventh chord may have **Three Progressions.**

The First progression, the most natural, is to the **Tonic Chord.**

Rules. The seventh descends one degree.

The fifth may ascend or descend; it generally descends.

The third must ascend one degree.

The root when at the bass ascends a fourth or descends a fifth, to the root of the tonic. When the chord is inverted the root is stationary.

It will be seen that the freedom of movement of common chords is lost when a dissonant is added, for the reason that they must move to a chord of which the note that the dissonant resolves on is a member.

Every possible arrangement of this progression is given here. Write in the same way the dominant seventh chords of the keys related to *C*, *taking care* to insert the necessary *accidentals* in every case.

Observe I, that when the Root is at the bass, the fifth of the Tonic has to be omitted. This is often avoided by omitting the third of the dominant and repeating the Root, thus:

or, by omitting the fifth, etc., (2).

II. The fifth is often made to ascend, when in the soprano or at the bass. When at the top in the third inversion, it may ascend to the third or to the fifth of the tonic.

III. When the Root of the dominant is at the top in the third inversion, it may ascend to the root of the Tonic. (It might do so when at the top in the other inversions, but does not sound so well.)

The introduction of this additional member of the dominant chord adds very much to our resources in harmonizing a melody, as any note in the melody may be harmonized as the seventh of a dominant, provided it is followed by the note on the next degree below, and provided it will be the seventh in one of the dominant chords of the Related Group.

In the above descending scale, harmonized twice, will be found all the dominant seventh chords of the group of *C*, and its relations, except one; viz., the dominant of *F*, the seventh of which is *B♭*. Observe that the third and seventh are the only notes in the scale which may not be sevenths.

The *B♭*, needed to make the seventh in the dominant of *F*, makes the fourth chromatically lowered note — (the others being, two belonging to the parallel minor, and the lowered supertonic).

For the present the lowered leading note of the scale must be harmonized as a dominant seventh.

Analyze the following example before writing the exercises that follow.

Proceed thus in analyzing:

First. Chord is tonic of key, quint position.

Second. Dominant of *A* minor, second inversion, third at top, followed by

Third. Tonic of *A* minor, octave position, mediant to the chord following.

Fourth. Dominant of *F* major, second inversion, seventh at top, followed by

Fifth. Tonic of *F*, tierce position.

Sixth. Dominant of *D* minor, second inversion, seventh at top, followed by

Seventh. Tonic of *D* minor, tierce position.

If any sequences are found point them out.

54 HARMONY.

I.

II.

III.

IV.

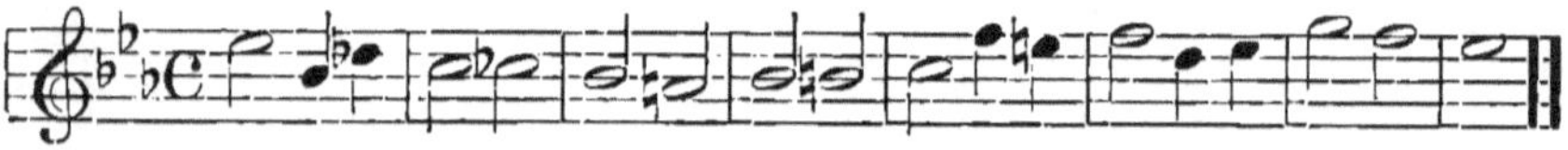

V.

VI.

VII.

There are a few exceptional cases in which the seventh does not descend in the first progression. They can only occur with the chords arranged exactly as follows.

1. The bass and top part ascending in thirds with each other.

2. Root at bass going to third, and seventh ascending to fifth. (This is more common in the older composers than it is now.)

3. Dominant, tierce position, followed by first inversion of Subdominant.

4. Diatonic scale in contrary motion.

5. Same, but the seventh is doubled; one ascends, the other descends.

Questions on Chapter XII.

What is a dissonant chord?
What is this movement called?
How are dissonant chords formed?
Which is the most important chord to which they may be added?
What is an essential dissonance?
What name is given to the series of dissonances that may be added to a given root?
What is the first addition to the dominant chord?
Of what kind is this seventh?
How does it resolve?
How many inversions may be made of a dominant seventh chord?
How many progressions may it have?
What is the first progression?
How do the members of the dominant seventh move in this progression?
When may the fifth of the dominant ascend?
When the root of the dominant seventh is at the bass, which member of the tonic following it must be omitted?
How may this omission be avoided?
When may a note in the melody be a seventh?
How many and which notes in the scale may be sevenths?
How must the chromatically lowered leading note be harmonized?
How many notes in the scale may be lowered accidentally?
Which are they, and how may they be harmonized?

CHAPTER XIII.

DOMINANT SEVENTH, SECOND AND THIRD PROGRESSIONS, AND SUCCESSION.

A dominant seventh chord may be repeated indefinitely, with changes in its position and inversion, provided that the dissonance is resolved when the **Progression** takes place. In the following example, the **Dominant** chord is struck four times before the progression to the **Tonic** takes place.

The **Second Progression** of the dominant seventh is to the **Submediant** (sixth of scale).

This progression only takes place with the **Root** of the **Dominant** at the bass.

The seventh and fifth descend. (The fifth must descend, otherwise it would make parallel fifths with the root.)

The **Third** ascends except when the fifth of the dominant is at the top. When this is the case it may descend.

The **Root** ascends to the root of the submediant.

1, 3, 5. Dominant seventh, followed by submediant.

2, 4, 6. Dominant seventh, followed by submediant of parallel minor.

In 5 the third descends, the fifth of the dominant being at the top.

Same in 6. This sounds better in instrumental than vocal music, owing to the awkward skip from B♮ to A♭.

Third Progression. The dominant seventh of a **Major Key** may be followed by the **Dominant** of its **Relative Minor.**

This progression may take place with any inversion.

The seventh descends; the fifth and third, being common to both chords, either remain stationary, or they may change places; that is, while one voice moves from the third to the fifth, another may reverse this, moving from the fifth to the third.

The **Root** ascends chromatically.

The seventh of the first chord may skip to the seventh of the second, while the fifth ascends to the **Root**; or the seventh may skip to the fifth of the second chord; last, the seventh may be omitted from the second chord.

1, 2, 3, 4. Third progression with root at bass and the three inversions.

5 and 6. Third and fifth changing places.

7. First inversion of one followed by second inversion of the other.

8. Seventh of first chord skipping to seventh of second chord.

9. Seventh of second chord omitted.

10. Seventh skipping to fifth of second chord.

Note. More will be said about this third progression in the chapter on chord of ninth.

It is necessary to observe that this progression may only be used with melodic passages that will permit of the resolution of the second chord as indicated by the small notes.

In addition to the **Three Progressions** of the dominant seventh chord, it is possible to make a **Succession** of dominant seventh chords, as follows:

The third of the chord, instead of being made to ascend, is lowered chromatically, and is made the seventh in the succeeding chord.

This **Succession** has the root and fifth, or third and seventh alternately at the bass; or all the chords may have the roots at the bass by omitting the fifth from every alternate chord.

1. Root stationary, fifth descends, root and fifth at bass.
2. Root stationary, fifth descends, third and seventh at bass.
3. Root at bass goes to root of next chord; the fifth is omitted from chords marked ×.

This succession should not be continued for more than two or three chords, as it soon grows monotonous.

Questions on Chapter XIII.

What is the second progression of dominant seventh?
How do the members of the chord move?
Which member of the dominant must be at the bass?
Does the third always ascend?
What is the third progression?
Can the dominant of a minor key have the third progression?
How do the members of the chord move in this progression?
What is it necessary to observe when using this progression?
How is a succession of dominant sevenths made?
How do the other members of the chord move?
What members of the chord may succeed each other as bass notes in this succession?
What must be omitted when the notes are at the bass?

HARMONY.

EXERCISES FOR ALL THE PROGRESSIONS AND THE SUCCESSION OF DOMINANT SEVENTHS.

Use third progression at the signs × ×.

CHAPTER XIV.

Dominant Ninth.

The next addition to the dominant chord is the **Ninth** over its root.
The ninth may be either Major or Minor.
Major ninth contains an octave and a whole-tone.
Minor ninth, an octave and a half-tone.
In Major keys both kinds of ninths are used.
In Minor keys the minor ninth only may be used.
The ninth resolves by descending one degree.
The ninth may not be used as a bass.
The ninth may not be written close to, or below the root; hence three inversions only may be made of this chord.
The fifth must ascend when below the ninth.
In four-part harmony, the third, fifth, or seventh may be omitted.
The first progression only is possible when the ninth is added.
The Succession of dominant chords may be made, provided the ninth is used only with alternate chords.
In general, the minor ninth sounds better than the Major when it is not at the top of the chord.

1. Dominant of *C*, with major ninth.
2. Dominant of *C*, with minor ninth.
3. First inversion. 4. Second inversion. 5. Third inversion.
6, 7, 8. The third omitted in 6 and 7, the ninth is minor, not being at the top of the chord.
9, 10. The fifth omitted.
11, 12, 13. The seventh omitted.

14. Succession of dominants. The ninth is not added to the second chord, but is to the third. If the succession were continued the fourth chord would be without the ninth. This example should be written in several keys.

We found (page 56) that it is possible to change the arrangement of a chord at will, and that there was no Progression until the harmony changed; but as the ninth in descending moves to the root of the chord, there may be **Resolution** without **Progression,** thus:

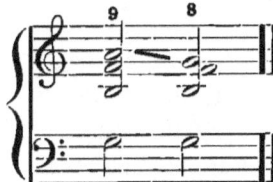

The ninth and seventh may also move freely to any other member of the chord before *progression* takes place.

1. Ninth leaps to seventh, then seventh to fifth.
2. Ninth ascends to third.
3. Ninth leaps up to seventh.
4. Seventh leaps up to ninth.

This shows that *resolution*, although it may (in the case of the ninth) take place without *progression*, is not compulsory.

The chord of the ninth is much used with the Root omitted. The remaining notes may be inverted in any form, and may have the *first* and *third* Progressions.

The omission of the root from a chord with Minor ninth makes it what is known as the **Diminished Seventh Chord.**

The fifth may descend in the diminished seventh chord when it is below the ninth, if the ninth is not at the top.

1. Third, fifth, seventh, major ninth, first progression.
2. Third, fifth, seventh, major ninth, third progression.
3. Third, fifth, seventh, minor ninth, called diminished seventh chord, because the interval from third to minor ninth is a diminished seventh.
4. Diminished seventh from dominant of *C*, and diminished seventh from dominant of *A*, its relative minor. Observe that three of the *letters* are common to both chords, and that the remaining sounds are enharmonically identical. It is owing to the fact of these two chords (viz., the dominant of any key, and the dominant of its relative minor) having so many sounds in common, that it is so easy to pass from one to the other.
5. *D*, the fifth, is at the bass and descends because *A♭*, the ninth, is not at the top.

Some more examples of the third progression.

1. First chord has seventh; the second, ninth without root.
2. Both chords have the ninth without root. Of course, in both these cases the notes that are common to both chords may change places in a variety of ways.

3 and 4. Give examples of the reversal of this progression. It is possible with other arrangements of the chords, but is most effective in the two here given.

HARMONY.

The study of the following example will give an idea of the wealth of harmonic possibilities there are in a given key and its relations, and we are by no means at the end of them yet.

Take as given key C; relative majors F, G; relative minors A, D, E.

1. The natural chords of the scale.
2. Chords from parallel minor.
3. Chord on lowered supertonic (during a modulation into a related key, *its* parallel minor and lowered supertonic may be used.)
4. Dominant harmony of the key.
5. The three groups derived from it.
6 and 7. Same in key of F.
8 and 9. Same in key of G.
10 and 11. Same in A minor.
12 and 13. Same in D minor.
14 and 15. Same in E minor.

Remember especially, that in using these dissonant chords no transition is made, because their **Tonics** are the **Natural Chords** of the **Given Key.** Observe also, that though there are several ways of harmonizing the chromatically lowered notes, they may all be ninths.

It would be time well spent to write out a number of tables like the preceding, taking care to get in the accidentals correctly.

Observe, that the seventh in the dominant of a major key is the ninth in the dominant of its relative minor; therefore all the notes in the scale that may be sevenths (Chapter XII.) may also be ninths on the same conditions.

Analyze the example that follows before writing the exercises. Give the name, root, and progression of every chord.

The succession of dominants may be made with diminished seventh chords. Mistakes are often made in writing this succession; but by applying the simple rule that the lowered third becomes the seventh in the next chord, and remembering the roots of these chords are the dominants of the related group, no mistake need occur. Observe that after writing six, all the dominant chords in the group, if you wish to continue the passage, return to the first chord — it being enharmonically the same as *A, C, E♭, G♭*, the chord that would follow *B♭, D♭, E, G*, according to the rule. In other words, when the lowering of the third will give a chord, the seventh of which is outside of the related group, substitute the diminished seventh chord belonging to the key of the mediant.

HARMONY.

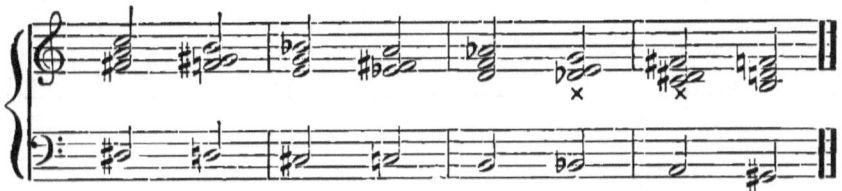

(This is treated at length not on account of its beauty, but because so many who *do* use it write it wrongly, overloading it with accidentals that should never appear in the key.)

Diminished seventh chords may move up as well as down (1); the seventh when at the bass may fall to the tonic (2).

Note. All examples and exercises should be played as well as written. This is the only way to learn to remember the *sound* by the *sight*, an absolute necessity to the composer.

EXERCISES INTRODUCING THE NINTH.

Use the ninth without the root more frequently than with it.

V.

VI.

Questions on Chapter XIV.

What is the next dissonant after the seventh that may be added to the dominant chord?
Is the ninth major or minor in major keys?
What is it in minor keys?
How does the ninth resolve?
May the ninth be used as a bass?
May the ninth be close to, or below the root?
How many inversions may be made of the ninth chord?
How must the fifth move?
May the fifth ever descend?
What members may be omitted in four-part harmony?
What progression may the ninth chord have?
How may the succession of dominant chords be made when the ninth is added?
What kind of ninth sounds best when it is not at the top?
In what form is this chord most frequently found?
What progressions are possible without the root?
What is the origin of the diminished seventh chord?
When may the fifth descend when below the ninth?
How many letters are common to the dominant of the major and the dominant of its relative minor? Which are they?
What sound have they in common? What member is it in each chord?
In what one way may all chromatically lowered notes be harmonized?

CHAPTER XV.

Chord of Dominant Eleventh.

The eleventh from the root is the next addition to the dominant chord. The third of the chord must be omitted.*

The movement of the eleventh is either down to the third, or up to the fifth.

The ninth moves with it or after it, when the eleventh descends; *with* it, when the eleventh ascends.

The remaining members of the chord are stationary, therefore no Progression takes place.

1. Eleventh and major ninth descending.
2. Eleventh and minor ninth descending.
3. Eleventh and major ninth ascending.

The major ninth may be changed to minor before descending to the root.

1. Major ninth descending after the eleventh.
2. Major ninth changed to minor before descending after the eleventh.
3. Eleventh stationary; often used in terminations.

As is the case with the seventh and ninth chords, so with the eleventh; leaps may be made freely from one member of the chord to another.

---

* Some weighty authorities say the third may be sounded with the eleventh. It is almost too harsh for sensitive ears.

The eleventh chord is much more used without, than with the root. The notes that remain, viz., the fifth, seventh, ninth, eleventh, may have the **Three Progressions** of the **Dominant. First Progression:**
The eleventh is stationary.
The ninth descends.
The seventh may go to any member of the tonic chord.
The fifth must ascend a second or a fourth.
The fifth, seventh, or ninth may be at the bass.

1. Fifth at bass ascends a second; seventh at top descends.
2. Fifth at bass ascends a second; seventh at top ascends.
3. Fifth at bass ascends a fourth; seventh at top descends. If it ascended here, the tonic would have no third.
4. Seventh at bass ascends to fifth of tonic; fifth at top ascends a second.
5. Seventh at bass descends to third of tonic; fifth at top ascends a second.
6. Seventh at bass descends to tonic; fifth at top ascends a fourth.
7. Seventh at bass falls to root of tonic; fifth at top ascends a second.
8. Ninth at bass.

Observe that all through *C* the eleventh does not move, as it is the root of the tonic.

In all these examples, *A*, the ninth, may be *A♭*, because the ninth may be major or minor in major keys.

Second Progression. (To Submediant, chord on sixth.) The eleventh and ninth are stationary; the seventh descends one degree; the fifth ascends one degree; the fifth or seventh may be at the bass.

Third Progression. (To dominant of relative minor.) Owing to the number of sounds common to these two chords (Chapter XIV.), this progression takes several forms; any of the notes may be at the bass.

1. Fifth at bass, ascends to root of dominant relative minor; eleventh, ninth, and seventh descend.
2. Fifth at bass, stationary; eleventh, ninth, seventh descend.
3. Fifth at bass; seventh and fifth stationary; eleventh and ninth descend.
4. Fifth at bass; ninth, seventh, fifth stationary; eleventh descends; result is that both are eleventh chords.

*This chord may have the same root as the preceding, in which case it would be third to ninth.

Write this progression out with every possible arrangement of the notes; also the first and second progressions with different arrangements of the upper notes.

The eleventh and ninth may descend while the seventh and fifth remain (as if the root were present), or the fifth may ascend to the root. In this last case, if the fifth is at the bass and ascends to the root of the dominant, the eleventh and ninth may ascend.

N. B. The descent of a fifth is always the same as the ascent of a fourth.

The following example gives in one view all the dominant harmonies so far, and tells how they may be distinguished.

a. Dominant of *C*, with added notes as far as the eleventh.

Broken into five groups of four sounds each.

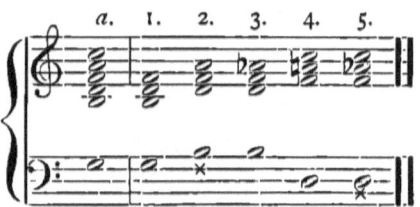

First group, counting from lowest note, consists of major third, perfect fifth, minor seventh; is therefore **Root to Seventh.**

Second group (counting as before) consists of minor third, diminished fifth, minor seventh; is therefore **Third to Major Ninth.**

Third group consists of minor third, diminished fifth, diminished seventh; is therefore **Third to Minor Ninth.**

Fourth group: minor third, perfect fifth, minor seventh; is therefore **Fifth to Eleventh,** with major ninth.

Fifth group is like 2; therefore a group consisting of minor third, diminished fifth, and minor seventh, may be either **Third to Major Ninth,** or **Fifth to Eleventh,** with minor ninth. To decide which it is, it is only necessary to remember what the roots of the dominant chords of the Related group are. Therefore *D*, *F*, *A♭*, *C*, if found in the key of *C*, must be fifth to eleventh, with minor ninth, because if it were third to major ninth, it is evident that *B♭* would be the root.

As to the other group, *B♭*, *D*, *F*, *A*, it may be *third to ninth,* dominant of *C,* or *fifth to eleventh* in the dominant of the relative minor of *C.*

Arrange the following groups in thirds, and find the roots. State to what keys they belong, and write their progressions.

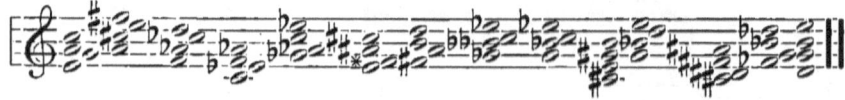

QUESTIONS ON CHAPTER XV.

What member of the chord must be omitted when the eleventh is added? How does the eleventh move?

What member moves with it?
Does the ninth always move with the eleventh?
In what way is this chord generally used?
What progressions may it have when the root is omitted?
What are the movements of the notes in the first progression?
What notes may be at the bass?
Give the movements of the notes in the second progression.
What may be at the bass?
Give movements of notes in third progression.
Which notes may be at the bass?
May eleventh and ninth move as if root were present?
How many groups of four sounds each may be derived from the dominant harmonies?
Of what intervals does the first group consist? The second? The third? The fourth? The fifth?
Which two groups are alike?
How may the roots of these similar groups be determined in a given key?
How must a group be arranged in order that the root may be found?

CHAPTER XVI.

Chord of Dominant Eleventh, Continued. Additional Remarks on Second Inversions.

In the following examples will be found the passages in which the eleventh is most frequently found.

1. Melody moves from first to third of major scale.
2. Melody moves from third to fifth of major scale.
3. Melody moves from first to third of minor scale.
4. Melody moves from third to fifth of minor scale.
5. Melody ascends from fifth of dominant to fifth of tonic.
6. This passage is frequent in terminations. In the last bar but one the seventh ascends instead of remaining stationary.

We have found that the succession of dominants might take place when ninth was added (page 64). It may also take place when eleventh is added.

1. First chord, *first to seventh*; second, *fifth to eleventh*.
2. First chord, *third to ninth*; second, *fifth to eleventh*.
3. First chord, *third to minor ninth* (at bass); second, *fifth to eleventh*.
4. Both chords, *fifth to eleventh*.
5. First chord, *fifth to eleventh*; second, *first to seventh*.
6. First chord, *fifth to eleventh*; second, *third to ninth*.

Observe that in *every* case the ninth may be major or minor.

All these progressions may be reversed.

The rule as first given for the Succession (page 58) may now be expressed as follows, since the succession may take place when the third is absent.

The harmonies of two or more roots descending by fifths may be written in succession.

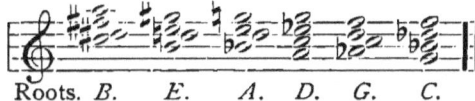

Harmonies from all the dominants of the related group in succession.

Additional Remarks on Second Inversions.

The second inversion of a chord may be followed by any chord with the same bass as that of the second inversion, or with a bass one degree above or below that of the second inversion. The second inversion of the tonic may be followed by the first inversion of the tonic.

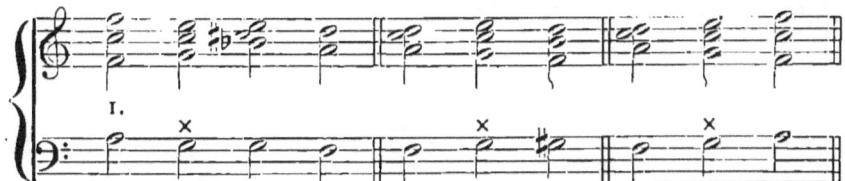

1. Second inversion of tonic, followed with various chords.
2. Second inversion of subdominant, followed by dominant.
3. Second inversion of dominant.
4. The chord of *A* minor, second inversion, enters as a tonic; but as it bears the relation of mediant to the key of *F*, advantage is taken of the fact that a second inversion may be followed by any chord with the same bass, and the dominant of *F* follows it.
5. Second inversion of tonic, changed to a dominant by the addition of the seventh to which the fifth skips.

EXERCISES FOR THE ELEVENTH CHORD.

In the first two the places are marked where an eleventh chord may be used.

CHAPTER XVII.

The Progressions of the dominant so far given, are the most natural and most usual; but successions may be made of which no *satisfactory* explanation can be given, in accordance with the following rule:

Any two of the Dominant Harmonies of the Related Group may be written in succession (with a few exceptions), provided they have at least one sound in common.

The dissonant notes are not always resolved in these successions, nor are these successions agreeable, except in certain arrangements of the chords.

The first thing to be done, is to find in which dominant harmonies each note in the scale may be found as root, third, fifth, seventh, ninth, or eleventh.

CONNECTING NOTE C.

Root. Seventh. Ninth. Eleventh.

C is root in dominant of *F*; seventh in dominant of *G*; ninth in dominant of *E* minor; eleventh in dominant of *C*.

CONNECTING NOTE D.

Root. Fifth. Seventh. Ninth. Eleventh.

D is root in dominant of *G*; fifth in dominant of *C*; seventh in dominant of *A* minor; ninth in dominant of *F*; eleventh in dominant of *D* minor.

Connecting Note E.

E is root in dominant of *A* minor; third in dominant of *F*; fifth in dominant of *D* minor; ninth in dominant of *G*; eleventh in dominant of *E* minor.

Connecting Note F.

F is seventh in dominant of *C*; ninth in dominant of *A* minor; eleventh in dominant of *F*.

Connecting Note G.

G is root in dominant of *C*; fifth in dominant of *F*; seventh in dominant of *D* minor; eleventh in dominant of *G*.

Connecting Note A.

A is root in dominant of *D* minor; fifth in dominant of *G*; seventh in dominant of *E* minor; ninth in dominant of *C*; eleventh in dominant of *A* minor.

Connecting Note B.

B is root in dominant of *E* minor; third in dominant of *C*; fifth in dominant of *A* minor.

78   HARMONY.

The chords marked × cannot be written in succession, although they have a connecting sound.

We give some examples below of these successions, in the arrangements which are most effective. The pupil should try other arrangements and should write them in various keys. No other exercise can equal this in giving the student a sure grasp of the possibilities of chord successions without *transition*.

The successions that come under rules already given are omitted, viz., the *third progression* (page 57), and the succession by lowering the third (page 58.)

CONNECTING NOTE C.

1. From *C*, *E*, *G*, *B*♭, to chords derived from *D*. This will serve as a model for all successions in which the connecting note is the *root* of the first group, and seventh in the second group.

2. Connecting note root and eleventh.

3. Connecting note, root and ninth.

4. Connecting note eleventh and seventh. This sounds well in any arrangement.

CONNECTING NOTE D.

As root and fifth, any arrangement, succession of dominants. As root and seventh, see Model (i. e., *C*, *E*, *G*, *B*♭, to derivatives of *D*).

1. Root and ninth; the second group may be either *third to ninth*, or *fifth to eleventh*. If considered as *third to ninth*, the root is dominant of *F*; if as fifth to eleventh, root is dominant of the relative minor of *F*.

Connecting Note E.

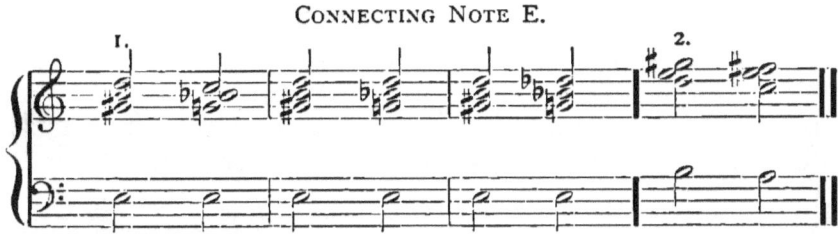

1. As root and third.
2. As root and ninth or eleventh (root of second chord, *D* or *B*).
As root and fifth, succession of dominants

Connecting Note F.

As seventh and ninth, third progression.   As seventh and eleventh.

Connecting Note G.

As root and fifth, succession of dominants.   As root and seventh.
(See Model.)

1. Gives an example of the *reversal* of the rule for the succession of dominants; i. e., *raised seventh* becoming third when the *root* of the first chord is present. First measure gives the arrangement that sounds best.
2. As root and eleventh.

Connecting Note A.

As root and fifth, succession of dominants.
As root and seventh.   (See Model.)

Connecting Note B.

As root and fifth, succession of dominants.

1. As root and third.

These examples, with two exceptions, only give the movements from the *first* chord to the others containing the same connecting note; but the movement may take place from *any* chord of the group to any other, with scarcely an exception. All the successions given may be reversed.

The two chords marked N. B. in the first example are identical in sound, because the diminished seventh derived from the dominant of a major key, and that derived from the dominant of its *relative minor*, are enharmonically the same, thus:

B, D, F, A♭, G♯, B, D, F.
Dominant of C, dominant of A minor.
E, G, B♭, D♭, C♯, E, G, B♭.
Dominant of F, dominant of D minor.
F♯, A, C, E♭, D♯, F♯, A, C,
Dominant of G, dominant of E minor.

The minor ninth in the dominant of the major is enharmonically the third in the dominant of its relative minor.

Observe in all these successions that the *connecting note* must remain in the *same part*.

The following successions in which there is no connecting note may be made.

HARMONY.

1 and 2. The second chord resolved as a dominant; in 2 the seventh falls to the root of the tonic.

3 and 4. Diminished seventh chord resolves as a supertonic harmony (Chapter XVIII.). It may resolve as a dominant, but the first is more agreeable.

EXERCISES FOR ELEVENTH CHORD, AND THE UNUSUAL PROGRESSIONS TREATED IN THE PREVIOUS CHAPTERS.

Eleventh may be used at ×. Look for opportunites for some of the successions given in last chapter. Where two notes in succession are marked × × there is an opportunity.

82   HARMONY.

CHAPTER XVIII.

Chord of Thirteenth.

In the majority of cases the thirteenth may, for practical purposes, be treated as a changing note, or as a retardation. Still there are some cases in which its movement is such that it must be looked upon as an essential dissonance.

The thirteenth, like the ninth, may be major or minor. The fifth is generally omitted when the thirteenth is added, especially in those cases in which the thirteenth descends to the twelfth (i. e., the fifth of the chord).

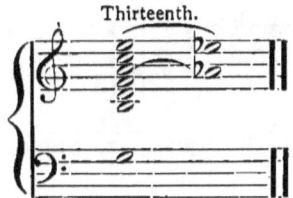

Dominant of *C*, with all the available overtones to the thirteenth.

In the examples that follow the cases are given in which the thirteenth may be looked upon simply as a changing note.

1. Root, third, seventh; *E* is the thirteenth, or a changing note.
2. Root, seventh, and ninth. 3. Third, seventh, and ninth.
4. Seventh, ninth, and eleventh. *A* may be flat or natural, at will. If all the *E*'s are made flat, the examples would be in *C* minor. In this case *A♭* would be necessary also.

5. *D♯* is a convenient mis-writing for *E♭*, the minor thirteenth.
(See remarks on augmented fifths.)

In the following examples it is not possible to look upon it as a changing note or retardation.

1. The thirteenth, *E*, falls to the root of the tonic. 2. Same, second progression.

3. Third progression, thirteenth falls to seventh of dominant of relative minor.

4. This looks like a second inversion of *E* minor. It is the only case in which a group of notes that form a common chord must be considered as a dominant group. From the manner of its entry it cannot be a second inversion of subdominant or dominant; and the strong upward tendency of the *B* proves that it is not a tonic, but a piece of dominant harmony.

5. Thirteenth stationary, seventh and ninth ascending to eighth and third.

6. Major ninth, eleventh, major thirteenth, resolving within the chord.

7. Major ninth, eleventh, minor thirteenth, resolving on tonic. Minor thirteenth ascends chromatically. (In this case the *E♭* is generally written *D♯*, making an augmented sixth chord.)

8. Same group with minor ninth and thirteenth resolved on tonic.

In this case the $E\flat$ must be used, as the combination of $A\flat$ and $D\sharp$ would be a monstrosity.

9. A succession of dominants, the first with minor thirteenth.
10. Same group as 8, resolving within the chord.
11. Dominant with minor thirteenth, followed by augmented sixth.
12. First chord, dominant, root, third, seventh, ninth; second chord, dominant, root and ninth having changed places; viz., bass, ninth; tenor, eleventh; alto, thirteenth; soprano, root. This passage is the only one in which the root may be struck over the ninth with good effect, owing possibly to the fact that the whole bar consists of dominant harmony, and also to the diatonic contrary motion.

In analyzing harmony a good rule to follow is, take the most obvious explanation, especially when the combinations may be "parsed" as common chords, instead of hunting for hidden "roots." For example, the following passage from Tannhauser is thus explained by one author. The note marked × is enharmonically $B\flat$, consequently is the ninth, $C\sharp$ the third, and $F\sharp$ the thirteenth in the dominant of D. But if it is looked on simply as the second inversion of $F\sharp$ major, changed to $F\sharp$ *minor*, and followed by the chord on the sixth (D major), a much simpler explanation may be given; viz., B minor, the preceding chord, is the minor subdominant of $F\sharp$, which enters as a *tonic;* second inversion is changed to minor, and followed by the chord on the sixth.

The beauty of the passage is owing largely to the uncertainty of key and the kaleidoscopic rapidity with which the changes of key take place.

The following passage, also by Wagner, the same author, calls an unusual form of augmented sixth, calling the $D\flat$ a miswriting for $C\sharp$, in spite of the fact that the C is natural *when the harmony changes.*

It is much easier to say it is the diminished seventh chord, dominant harmony of $B\flat$. The $D\flat$ is a changing note which leaps to another member of the chord, then runs to its resolution, C. The chord $A\natural$, C, $E\flat$, $G\flat$, is enharmonically $F\sharp$, A, C, $E\flat$, a derivative of the chord that follows. It follows that in both instances Wagner wrote his chords properly.

Chord of eleventh, dominant of $B\flat$.   Eleventh resolved.

The best way to become familiar with this chord is to transpose the examples into all the keys.

CHAPTER XIX.

SUPERTONIC HARMONY.

There is another progression of dissonant groups, that differs so widely from any that they have as **Dominant** harmonies, that to distinguish them they are called **Supertonic Harmonies,** from the fact that their progression is to the **Tonic** chords of the keys in which their **Roots** are the **Supertonics.**

The major ninth is stationary. The minor ninth ascends chromatically in **Major** keys, is stationary in minor keys. (The major ninth cannot be used in minor keys.)

The seventh is stationary.

The fifth and third go to the fifth of the Tonic.

The root when at the bass goes to the fifth of the Tonic; when not at the Bass, to the third of the Tonic generally, but it may go to the fifth.

1. Supertonic harmony of *C*, with major ninth stationary.
2. Supertonic harmony of *C*, with minor ninth ascending chromatically.
3. Supertonic harmony of *A* minor, with minor ninth stationary. As the root, third, and fifth all go to the fifth of the tonic, it will at once be seen that the second inversion of the tonic generally follows.

1. *First inversion*, with root present.
2. *First inverson*, root omitted, major ninth.

3. *First inversion*, root omitted, minor ninth.
4. *Second inversion*, root present.
5. *Second inversion*, root omitted, major ninth.
6. *Second inversion*, root omitted, minor ninth.

7. When the root is at bass it is generally repeated, and the fifth is omitted.

8. When the third is at bass and the ninth is minor, the third may fall to the root of the tonic.

1. When the seventh is at the bass, it is generally repeated when the ninth is at top.

2. Minor ninth, fifth at top.

3 and 4 give the usual way of writing these two chords; viz., with $D\sharp$ instead of $E\flat$.

5. Has the minor ninth at bass.

The supertonic harmony may be preceded by the eleventh chord.

Also by the first inversion of the chord on lowered supertonic. This is the only case in music in which it is possible to write in succession chords arising from two forms of the same root; viz., $D\flat$, F, $A\flat$, and $D\natural$, $F\sharp$, $A\natural$.

HARMONY.

The eleventh of the supertonic harmony may be used. It sounds best with the minor ninth.

1 and 2. Fifth at the bass.
3. Minor ninth at the bass.
4. Seventh at the bass.

Questions on Chapter XIX.

What distinguishes the supertonic harmony from the dominant?
How does the major ninth proceed? The minor ninth in major keys? The minor ninth in minor keys? The fifth? The third? The root, when at bass? The root, when not at bass?
In what form does the tonic generally follow it?
Which members of this chord are used when the root is at the bass?
Does the third always ascend? When may it not?
Give the rule for use of seventh as a bass.
What miswriting is often used in this case?
May the eleventh of supertonic be used?

Exercises on Supertonic Harmony.

When the second inversion of tonic follows the supertonic harmony, be careful to follow it according to rule.

CHAPTER XX.

Altered Chords, Augmented Sixth, Augmented Fifth, Passing Seventh.

There are a few chords that are produced by altering one of the members of a given chord, chromatically.

Strictly considered, this altered note is nothing but a passing note between the member of the chord and the note to which this member moves.

The most important of these chords by alteration is called the **Augmented Sixth Chord.**

This Chord results from the chromatic lowering of the fifth of a dominant or supertonic harmony, *root to seventh* or *third to minor ninth*.

The progression of the chord is unchanged. It may be inverted in any way, but the chromatically lowered fifth is generally used as a bass.

The chord gets its name from the fact that the interval between the lowered fifth and the third of the chord is an **Augmented Sixth**; thus, D, $A\flat$, $F\sharp$.
   Root, Fifth, Third.

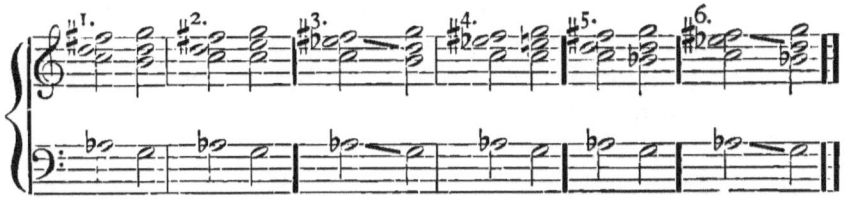

1. Progressing like a dominant, root present.
2. Progressing like a supertonic harmony, root present.

3 and 4. Same as 1 and 2, but the root is omitted and minor ninth added.

5 and 6. Progressing like a dominant to a *minor* tonic. This pro-

gression of the augmented sixth is unusual. When it progresses like a dominant, the chord to which it moves is (generally) also a dominant.

The parallel fifths that occur in 3 and 6 are not at all unpleasant. They may be found in the best writers.

The following inversions of the augmented sixth are used.

1. The upper notes may be arranged in any way; the seventh of the original chord is at the bass.

2. Minor ninth at the bass.

3. Third at bass. 2 and 3 sound best when arranged as here given.

The rule for the succession of dominant chords by lowering the third chromatically applies to this chord.

1. Root present. 2. With minor ninth. The $E\flat$ is suspended to avoid the parallel fifths between the outer parts.

The minor ninth may be resolved and the lowered fifth restored at the same time.

1. The ninth at top, lowered fifth at bass.

2. The ninth at bass, lowered fifth at top. This progression is of singular beauty. It is often incorrectly written; viz., the $A\flat$ written $G\sharp$, or the $F\sharp$ written $G\flat$.

3. The same, but with the third lowered, making a succession to *fifth, seventh, ninth, eleventh,* dominant of *C.* Then the ninth ($A\flat$) of this chord is resolved, and the fifth at the same time lowered.

Rewrite the exercises on supertonic harmony, substituting an augmented sixth whenever the supertonic harmony was used (except with the notes marked ×).

Questions on Chapter XX.

How is the chord of augmented sixth formed?
What progressions has it?
Which member of the chord is generally used as a bass?
Between which two members of the chord does the interval of the augmented sixth lie that gives the chord its name?
Is the succession by lowering the third possible with this chord?

Chord of Augmented Fifth.

This chord may be produced in two ways: —
First, by chromatically raising the fifth of a Major chord.
Second, by chromatically lowering the root of a Minor chord.
The raised fifth must ascend; any chord may follow that includes the note to which the raised fifth ascends.
The fifth of the Dominant chord in Major keys may be raised when the seventh is added; in general the raised fifth is put above the seventh.

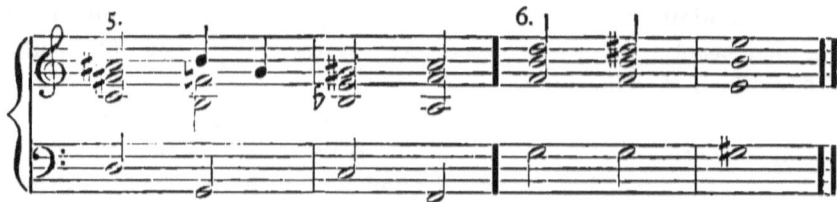

1. *C* with augmented fifth, root at bass.
2. *C* with augmented fifth, third at bass.
3. *C* with augmented fifth, fifth at bass.
4. Dominant seventh, with augmented fifth.
5. *Succession*, first and third chords, with augmented fifth.
6. Dominant of *C*, augmented fifth, third progression.

The augmented fifth chord, produced by lowering the root of a minor chord, is always followed by either the second inversion of the tonic (Example 1), or by the dominant (Example 2) of its relative major.

It is never inverted, being quite ineffective except with the root at the bass.

What is known as the chord of **Passing Seventh** may be conveniently included in this group of chords with passing tones.

The passing seventh may be added to any chord; it may be either Major or Minor; it always descends.

1. Tonic, with passing seventh.
2. Subdominant, with passing seventh.

3. Mediant, with passing seventh.

4. Submediant, with passing seventh. In this case the seventh is at the bass, as the chord may be inverted just as a dominant seventh is. In fact, it will be seen that it progresses exactly like a dominant seventh; thus, *first, third, fourth, fifth* resemble dominant, followed by tonic; 2 is like a dominant with second progression.

5. Tonic with passing seventh, with fifth at bass.

When the passing seventh is Major, which is only so with the **Tonic** and **Subdominant** chords, the augmented fifth is often used with it.

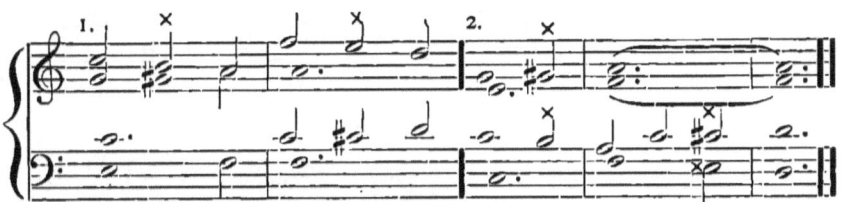

The use of the Augmented fifth furnishes a new way of treating *raised* notes. The only one that may not be so treated, without going outside the Related Group, is the raised fourth. It enables us to raise the sixth of the scale, thus:

Questions on Chapter XX. (Continued.)

How may the chord of the augmented fifth be produced?
How does the raised fifth move?
What chords may follow the augmented fifth?
May the fifth be augmented in the dominant seventh chord? In both major and minor keys?
How is this chord generally arranged?
By what chords may the augmented fifth chord, produced by lowering the root of a minor chord, be followed?

May this augmented fifth chord be inverted? May the former one?
To what chords may the passing seventh be added?
How does it move?
Is it major or minor?
May a chord with passing seventh be inverted?
What chord does it resemble in its progressions?
In which chords is the passing seventh major?
What may be used with it in these cases?
Which raised notes in the scale may be treated as augmented fifths?
What *new* raised note may be introduced as an augmented fifth?

EXERCISES FOR AUGMENTED FIFTH AND PASSING SEVENTH.

HARMONY.

CHAPTER XXI.

SUSPENSIONS.

(*Note.* *Suspension* and *Retardation* are treated in a new way in this work, the intention being to bring out clearly the difference between them.)

The seventh and ninth, Major or Minor, may be added to any common chord by **Suspension**; i. e., by tying the note that becomes the seventh or ninth from a preceding chord in which it is a consonant member (root, third, or fifth).

The Suspended seventh and ninth resolve by descending one degree. The remaining notes follow the rules given for the progression of the dominant seventh and ninth (*q. v.*).

The rule may be put thus: the root of the chord in which the suspended seventh is resolved is always the fourth above, second above, or third below that of the chord in which the suspension occurs.

1. Chord of *E*, with suspended seventh (*D*); root ascends a fourth (like first progression of dominant seventh).
2. Same; root ascends a second (like second progression of dominant seventh).
3. Root (*C*) is third below (like third progression of dominant seventh).

Diatonic sequences may be made, in which every chord has a suspended seventh.

Any Diatonic Sequence may be turned into an harmonic sequence. The above may be changed to the succession of dominant sevenths (by lowered thirds).

The suspended seventh may be inverted like the dominant seventh.

The suspension belongs more to the old diatonic or contrapuntal system than to the harmonic.

CHAPTER XXII.

Retardation.

When a note is prolonged from a chord in which it is a member, into one in which it is not a member, thus becoming dissonant, it is called a **Retardation** of the member of the second chord upon which it resolves.

The **Retardation** differs from the **Suspension** in the following respects:

First, there is no change in the harmony when it resolves.

Second, the **Suspended** seventh and ninth are always found in conjunction with a common chord, while the retardation may take place in any group.

Third, the **Suspension** is always prepared by a consonant member of some chord, viz., root, third, or fifth, while a **Retardation** may be made by prolonging any member of a chord, consonant or dissonant.

Fourth, **Suspensions** always resolve by **Descending**, while **Retardations** may either **Ascend** or **Descend**.

The member of the *first* chord is the *Preparation;* the tied note (or repeated note) is the *Retardation*.

The member of the *second* chord (that follows the tied note) is the *Resolution* or *Retarded note*.

When a Retardation resolves by *descending*, its descent may be a whole or half-tone. When it resolves by *ascending* it must be a half-tone when the note to which it ascends is the root or fifth of the chord; if it ascends to the third it may be a whole or half-tone.

The note upon which a Retardation resolves may be repeated in a lower part, but not in a part *above* the Retardation. (Frequent exceptions to this last rule may be found, but they rarely, if ever, sound well.)

1, 2, 3. Retardation of the root from above; the second chord has root, then third, then fifth at the bass.

4, 5, 6. Retardation of root from below, etc.

7, 8, 9. Retardation of third from above.

10, 11, 12. Retardation of third from below.

13, 14, 15. Retardation of fifth from above.

16. Retardation of fifth from below.

This Retardation may take place only in this progression; viz., from supertonic harmony or augmented sixth to tonic.

17. Seventh retarded from below.

18. Retardation of seventh from above. In this the root (G) is above the ninth (A). This is possible only when it is used as a retardation of the seventh.

Two or three members of a chord may be retarded at the same time.

1. Root and third, retardation from above.
2. Root below, third above.
3. Root and third from below.
4. Root and third from above.
5. Root, third, and fifth from above.
6. Root from below, third and fifth from above.
7. Root from above and below, third and fifth from above.

The next example gives the retardation in the bass, first of the third from above. This is the best, because it is not necessary to have the retarded note repeated in an upper voice, as is the case with 2 and 3.

2 and 3 belong more properly to that kind of syncopation in which one or more parts drag behind the rest, as follows:

The bass may move to another member of the chord at the same time the retardation resolves, or before it.

In the examples which follow will be found a series of sevenths treated in three ways, which will serve to make the difference between **Suspension** and **Retardation** clear.

1 is a sequence which may be considered as a series of first inversions with **Retardation** of the roots.

2 is a sequence of real **Suspended Sevenths.**

3 is so harmonized that the seventh over the bass is in turn the Retardation of every member of a chord from root to ninth.

In 3, at *a*, the root (*G*) becomes a retardation of the seventh (*F*), because the ninth (*A♭*) is below it. This is the only way in which the ninth may be sounded below the root. *b*. The third is retarded. At *c* the fifth; at *d* the root; at *e* the third; and at *f* the ninth (*A*) is retarded by the prolongation of *B* (the third) over *C*

HARMONY.

(the eleventh). This is the only way in which the third and eleventh may be sounded together (with the third above).

Questions on Chapter XXII.

What is a retardation?
In what respect does it differ from a suspension?
What accompanies a suspension? What a retardation?
How is a suspension prepared? How a retardation?
How does a suspension resolve? How a retardation?
When a retardation descends, what may the interval be?
When it ascends?
When may the note of resolution be repeated?
May double retardations occur? Triple?
What retardations are possible at the bass?
What movement may the bass make?

104   HARMONY.

Rewrite the following succession of chords with as many retardations as possible.

Proceed as follows:

Suspensions and **Retardations** do not always move directly to their Resolution, but postpone it by the introduction of certain other notes. This is called Ornamentation of the Dissonances. A Suspended seventh or ninth may ascend one degree, then fall a third to the resolution (Example 1); or may fall a third, then ascend one degree to the resolution (Example 2).

In both cases the descent of a third may be filled by adding the intermediary note (Examples 3 and 4).

The same ornamentation may be given to a descending Retardation (Example 1).

An ascending Retardation may leap to the note above, then fall to its resolution (Example 2); or the ascent of a third may be filled as in the preceding cases. Lastly, an ascending or descending retardation may leap to any member of the chord in which it occurs, before going to its resolution (Example 3); and the interval from the retardation to this note, or from this note to the resolution, may be changed to a run (Example 4.)

The ornamentation may be varied in many ways, but the underlying principle is always the same; viz., a movement from one side to the other of the Resolution note, upon which the dissonance finally comes to rest, varied by a leap or run to some other member of the chord.

1. Retardation falls to another note of the chord, then leaps back to the dissonance.

2. Same, but runs up to note below resolution, then leaps to note above it.

3. Descends to note below resolution.

4. Runs to note above resolution.

5. There are two chords in this bar: first, F, A, C, is implied; the

E is at first a retardation of *F*, then of *D* in chord *D*, *F*, *A*. From this it may be seen that the *passing* seventh (Chapter XIX.), although itself a dissonance, may be used to prepare another dissonance. .

6. Leap to another member of chord, then to note below and note above resolution.

7. Leap to note below, then to another member of chord, from which it runs down to the resolution.

Double Retardations may be ornamented, provided they move together in thirds or sixths, or provided the same variety of ornamentation is applied to both.

QUESTIONS ON CHAPTER XXII. (CONTINUED.)

Do suspensions and retardations always move directly to their resolution?
What is this introduction of other notes called?
Describe the various kinds of ornamentation that both suspensions and retardations may have.
May the passing seventh be used to prepare a retardation?
May double retardations be ornamented?

EXERCISES ON ORNAMENTED SUSPENSIONS AND RETARDATIONS.

II.

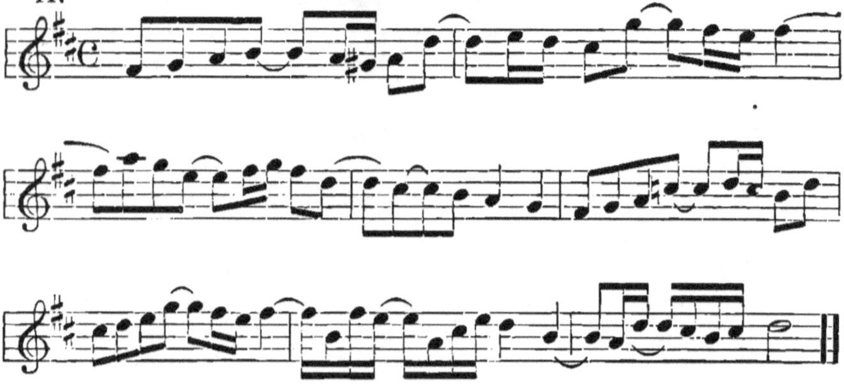

III.

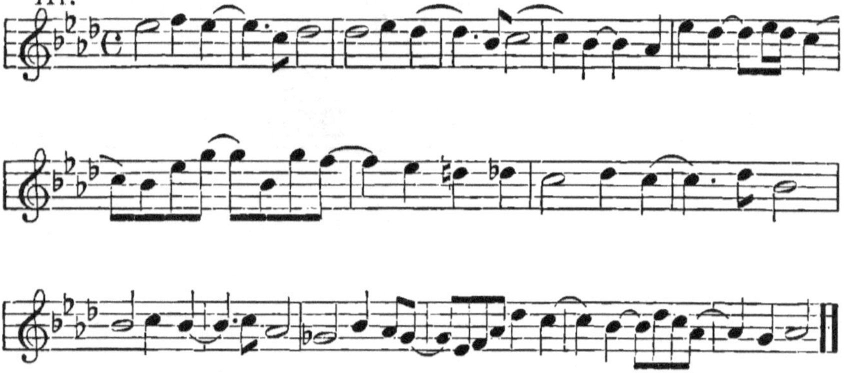

The augmented fifth may be used as a preparation of a retardation.

IV.

CHAPTER XXIII.

Changing Notes or Appoggiaturas.

These differ from Retardations only in being Struck instead of being Prolonged from a preceding chord. They fall on the accented beats, or if there are two notes or more to the beat, on the first of each beat.

They may fall on an unaccented beat if the accompanying harmony is syncopated.

When below the member of the chord upon which they resolve, they must be a half-tone below it, except when they occur as part of an ascending diatonic scale.

All accidentally raised notes that fall on the accented beats, or on the first note of a beat, may be treated as **Changing Notes**, when they ascend one degree.

They may be doubled in thirds and sixths like Retardations.

1. On accented beats.
2. On first note of beat.

3. On second beat (unaccented), the harmony syncopated.

4. The *D*, a whole-tone below *E*. Like the retardation, the changing note may be a whole-tone below the third of a chord.

5. Raised notes on first of beat.

6. Doubled in thirds and sixths.

7. Same, with raised notes.

A Dominant harmony may be struck over the root or third of the tonic, making Double, Triple, or Quadruple Changing Notes. The dominant harmony moves according to the rule (1) and (2).

A changing note below the *third* and one above the fifth of a common chord may be struck over the root, or root and fifth (3) and (4.)

The **Changing Note** may be ornamented like the Retardation.

HARMONY.

Questions on Changing Notes.

1. In what respect do changing notes differ from retardations?
2. On which beat of the measure do they fall?
3. May they occur in any other situation?
4. When do they fall on an unaccented beat?
5. When may they be a whole-tone below the note of resolution?
6. When may accidentally raised notes be treated as changing notes?
7. May changing notes be doubled?

Exercises on Changing Notes.

The note upon which the **Changing Note** resolves may not be struck with it, but it may be struck at the octave below.

I.

II.

III.   Ornamented Changing Notes.

CHAPTER XXIV.

Passing Notes.

The last manner in which Dissonant unharmonized notes may be used is, as **Passing Notes.**

Passing Notes occur *between* the harmonies on the unaccented beats, or on the second note of the beat.

There are **Five Varieties.**

The **First Variety** enters by degrees forming part of an ascending or descending diatonic or chromatic scale. To get a passing note of this variety there must be at least three ascending or descending notes in succession, the middle one of which may be a passing note.

a. The *A* must ascend and double the third (*B*) in the next chord, to avoid making the parallel fifths, *A*, *E*, *G*, *D*.

b. The third (*E*) is doubled here, because if the root (*C*) were doubled it would clash with the passing note (*D*).

c. This is the only way in which a note may be natural and sharp at the same time. (Theoretically this should be D♭, but for all practical purposes it is more convenient to treat it as a chromatic passing note.)

Diatonic or chromatic scales of any length may be played with a single chord, provided the first and last, or second and last notes are members of the chord. If the second and last are members of the chord, the first note is a **Changing Note.** In passages of this kind it is convenient to consider all the intervening notes as passing notes. The chord may be changed with the last note.

The direction of the scale may be changed whenever a note belonging to the chord is reached, or the scale may be abandoned when such a note is reached.

a. In the first measure each time a member of the chord is reached, the motion is changed, the next group of sixteenths beginning with a changing note.
b. The change of direction *begins* with the member of the chord.
c. Is a passing note of the second variety.
d. The scale is abandoned. There is a leap from one member to another of the chord.

The **Second Variety** enters by degrees above or below the harmonized note, but returns to the same note. All varieties of turn, trill, mordent are founded on this variety.

Like the Retardations this variety of passing note, when *below* the harmonized note, sounds better if a half-tone; but it *may* be a whole-tone below the third of a chord.

The **Third Variety** enters by a leap from one harmonized note to the degree above or below the next harmonized note.

When below it must be a half-tone. All accidentally raised notes that occur on the unaccented beats, or the second member of the beat, may be treated as passing notes of this variety.

The **Fourth Variety** may be described as an Ornamented Diatonic scale, made by adding to each note of the scale the note above or below, or a third above or below. So many variations may be made in this variety that it is only possible to give a few examples.

Some apparently elaborate passages may be reduced to very simple harmonic elements by eliminating the passing notes; for example, the following from Handel.

The **Fifth Variety** is called the **Anticipating Note**. It just reverses the Retardation; i.e., it anticipates the following chord by sounding one of its members before the preceding chord is left.

In the example that follows, all these varieties are used in a cadenza-like passage over a single chord.

Observe that every change in the direction of the motion begins with a member of the chord.

All the ornamentation that may be given to the retardation and the changing note may be given to the first three varieties of the passing note.

1. First variety, leaping to note below.
2. To another member of the chord.
3. Second variety, leaping to note below.
4. To another member of the chord.
5. Third variety, leaping to note above.
6. Leaping to note below.

The first three varieties may be doubled in thirds and sixths (1).

The first (diatonic) may also be doubled at the octave or third, when moving in opposite directions (2).

The second and third varieties may be doubled at augmented fourth or diminished fifth (like changing notes) (3).

A diatonic scale of first inversions may be written over a single note or chord (4).

Diatonic or chromatic scales may be written in contrary motion, in either single notes, thirds, or sixths, provided the first and last notes struck together belong to the same harmony (5).

A passing note is sometimes followed by a changing note (6).

The resolution of a passing note is sometimes retarded by repeating it (7); or by leaping to some other member of the chord and returning to the passing note (8).

HARMONY.

Third Sonata. Beethoven.

Examples may be found of changing and passing notes used in a manner that does not conform to any of the rules here given, but they are rare, and will cause the pupil no difficulty if these rules are well understood.

QUESTIONS ON PASSING NOTES.

What is a passing note?
How many varieties are there of passing notes?
Describe the first variety.
How many notes must there be in succession to have a passing note of this variety?
How may extended diatonic and chromatic scales be treated?
Describe the second variety of passing note.
Describe the third variety?
When may accidentally raised notes be treated as passing notes?
Describe the fourth variety.
Describe the fifth variety.
May the ornamentation used with retardations and changing notes be applied to passing notes?
To all varieties?
In what ways may passing notes be doubled?

EXERCISES ON PASSING NOTES AND CHANGING NOTES.

CHAPTER XXV.

FURTHER REMARKS ON THE MINOR SCALE.

(It was necessary to defer this chapter until changing and passing notes were explained.)

The changeable notes in the minor scale offer some difficulties to the student. The following instructions will make this point clear.

In scale passages ascending, either the harmonic or melodic form may be used when accompanied by the tonic chord (1).

When accompanied by the subdominant chord, the harmonic or natural form may be used (2).

When accompanied by the dominant, root to seventh, the melodic or harmonic form; but if the dominant harmony is *third to ninth*, or *fifth to eleventh*, the harmonic form must be used (3).

Descending scale, tonic chord accompanying, use natural or harmonic (4).

Subdominant accompanying, use natural form (5).

Dominant accompanying, use harmonic form (6).

The form given in 7 is much used by Bach and Handel. It differs from the major scale only in having a minor third above the tonic.

The raised sixth of the minor scale, when in the melody, may be harmonized as in the example following, 1; when in the bass, 2. These both belong to the old school of music. Some writers say that 2 should never be used, but 3, from the "Duetto" (Songs Without Words), is a sufficient argument for its use. 4 and 5 give the usual ways of harmonizing it. 6. It is treated as a passing note on the tonic chord. 7. It is treated as a changing note in the dominant chord.

The natural seventh descending: 1. Diatonic harmony, rugged but effective on occasion. 2. The same passage in the bass. This manner of using the first inversion of the minor chord on the dominant, viz., when the bass descends diatonically from the keynote to the sixth or fifth of the scale, is very effective. Some authors say it is the only way this chord may be used, in spite of the fact that self-willed composers often use it otherwise with excellent effect. 3 and 4 give modern ways of harmonizing this note. 5 and 6 give examples of the use of the raised sixth in descending passages; in 5 the sixth returns to the seventh. In 6 the sixth and seventh are both raised, although in a descending passage; the seventh because the harmony requires it, the sixth to avoid the skip of augmented second, which is very disagreeable in the bass.

The augmented fifth on the third degree of the minor scale may be used. It is generally used as a retardation, (1).

2 shows how the natural seventh may be used as a passing or changing note with the raised seventh.

EXERCISES IN MINOR KEYS.

I.

The relations of a minor key are those related to its relative major.

CHAPTER XXVI.

Open or Vocal Harmony.

The way in which the exercises have been written so far is called Close Harmony; i. e., the three upper parts are kept as close together as possible.

This has been done because it is the easiest way in which chord successions may be written, and because of a belief that after the pupil has *learned* the chords and the rules that govern their motions, the writing of them in Open or Vocal score is very much easier than when the pupil has not only the rules for open harmony, but also for the formation and succession of the chords to remember at the same time.

Any correctly written example of chords in *Position* may be turned into Open Harmony by the simple expedient of moving the middle note of the upper three down an octave, thus:

This expedient fails when Inversions and Dissonant chords are used; for example, the following is right in close harmony, but when written in open, three successive fifths will be found at *a*, and a poor arrangement of the voices at *b*, the tenor and bass being too close, and the soprano and alto too far apart.

Rules. All previous rules as to Progression and Resolution must be strictly observed.

No two parts must ever move together in Octaves, Fifths, or Unisons.

Avoid the following leaps: *augmented second, fifth, sixth; diminished third, fourth;* major seventh, minor seventh; except when from root to seventh of dominant chord, all leaps beyond the octave.

Avoid *all* long leaps in the Inner parts (Alto and Tenor). Never allow the Alto and Tenor to be separated by an interval greater than an octave.

Keep the voices within the following limits, using the highest and lowest notes of each voice rarely.

This kind of writing should also be practised on four staves (one for each voice). It is customary now to use the *G* clef for the Tenor, with the understanding that its pitch is an Octave Lower than when used for the Soprano.

The example (marked *A*), page 124, is here given on four staves.

Rewrite all, or as many as possible of the preceding exercises, except those on changing and passing notes, in open harmony, after studying the following examples. This department belongs more especially to the study of counterpoint.

Observe that when a note belongs to two or more chords in succession, it may be written as a single note equalling the others in value; as in second measure, first example.

When a letter is altered by a sharp, flat, or natural, keep it in the same voice.

CHAPTER XXVII.

Pedal or Organ Point.

By this is meant the prolongation of a single sound through several measures, generally in the lowest part, while a succession of harmonies related to the key is written over it.

These harmonies must be written as though the **Pedal Note** were not present. But the **Pedal Note** must be a member of at least the first and last chords.

The Dominant is most frequently used as a pedal; next, the Tonic; next, the Tonic and Dominant together.

Examples of other degrees of the scale used as pedals are rare. Examples may be found of tonic, dominant, and the fifth of the dominant (i. e., the supertonic) used together.

Progressions may be written with the greatest freedom over the Dominant; next, over the Tonic.

They are necessarily much restricted when both these notes are used, and still more when the three notes mentioned above are used.

If the prolonged note is a member of all the chords written over it, viz., root or fifth, it is not strictly speaking a **Pedal**. This kind of prolonged note is often used in an upper part. (The real Pedal is rarely so used, and the harmonies that may be written with it are much restricted.)

In Pianoforte and Orchestral music the Pedal note is often repeated or alternated with its octave, or with the half-tone below it.

A succession consisting of the Tonic, Dominant, and Tonic is often written over the Tonic, which might then be termed a Pedal of short duration.

128   HARMONY.

1. Dominant Pedal.
2. Tonic Pedal.
3. Tonic and Dominant together.
4. Tonic, Dominant, and Supertonic. This is rarely used unless a quasi rustic effect is desired. It must end by the supertonic falling to the octave of the tonic.
5. Example of a prolonged note that is a member of every chord, therefore not strictly a pedal.

1. The Pedal repeated, alternated with its octave and with the half-tone below.

2. Pedal on the tonic, of short duration.

3. Is a beautiful illustration of this variety of pedal, from Chopin's Cradle Song. This accompaniment persists all through the piece. It is simply a breaking or dispersion of the following chords.

Pedals of considerable length may be met with in which transitions are made to non-related keys, but as a rule the harmonies are confined to the **Related Group.**

CHAPTER XXVIII.

Transition.

Transition is the act of passing out of the related group.

A **Transition** is not established until a **Tonic Chord** foreign to the **Group** is struck.

The presence of a *Tonic* chord may be indicated in two ways: first, and most emphatically, by being preceded by the harmony of its own dominant; second, by appearing in its Second Inversion, provided the second inversion does not enter in the manner prescribed for a second inversion of dominant or subdominant.

As this second means of making a Transition does not necessitate the use of Dissonant chords, we will begin with it.

Taking first the Major chords in the scale, each one may be a **Tonic** without transition.

The first and fourth may be **Subdominants** without Transition; but if the fifth is treated as a Subdominant, and is followed by the second inversion of its **Tonic**, it gives a transition, thus:

The chord *G*, *B*, *D* is treated as subdominant of *D*, and is followed by the second inversion of *D*, which is outside of the group.

The three major chords may also be dominants; the first and fifth within the group, the fourth gives a transition, thus:

F, *A*, *C*, as dominant, followed by *B*♭, *D*, *F*, out of the group.

A major chord is also found on the sixth degree of the minor scale. Of the three major chords in *C*, the first and fourth treated thus remain within the group, but the fifth passes out of the group, thus:

G, B, D is treated as sixth in *B* minor.

Transition by treating the major chord as sixth in a minor scale may be extended by treating the Minor scale as the parallel of a Major scale, thus:

1. *C, E, G,* as sixth of *E* minor, the parallel of *E* major.
2. *F, A, C,* as sixth of *A* minor, the parallel of *A* major.
3. *G, B, D,* as sixth of *B* minor, the parallel of *B* major.

A major chord may also be treated as being the chord on the Lowered Supertonic of either a Major or Minor scale, thus:

1. *C, E, G,* as lowered supertonic of *B,* Major or Minor.
2. *F, A, C,* as lowered supertonic of *E,* Major or Minor.
3. *G, B, D,* as lowered supertonic of *F♯,* Major or Minor.

For the sake of clearness the Tonic of the key to which the **Transition** is made follows directly after the chord by *means* of which the Transition is made, but as a result of the rule already given, that the movement of common chords is perfectly free, any of the chords belonging to the new scale may appear before the tonic is struck. For example, *C, E, G,* is found in *C,* as tonic; *F,* as dominant, *G,* as subdominant. It may therefore be followed by any chord in these keys or their related keys. But when treated as sixth of a parallel minor, or as a lowered supertonic, it is subject to the rules already given for the use of these chords (Chap. XI.).

The three *Minor* chords in the scale, treated as tonics, remain within the related group.

As subdominants, those on the second and sixth remain within, unless treated as belonging to parallel minor scales, thus:

1. *D, F, A,* subdominant, *A* minor, parallel of *A* major.
2. *A, C, E,* subdominant, *E* minor, parallel of *E* major.
3. *E, G, B,* subdominant, *B* minor; gives a Transition when followed by either B major or minor.

A Minor chord is also found on the third of the major scale. The supertonic is the only one that will give a transition when treated this way.

In the following example all the transitions are made by means of common chords, treated in the various ways just pointed out. The

HARMONY.

places where the transitions occur are marked. It is left to the pupil to explain them.

N. B. The chords of $C\sharp$ and $D\flat$ are enharmonically the same.

Transition by means of **Dominant Harmonies.**
Any Dominant Harmony may be followed by either a major

or minor tonic. Thus the following groups derived from G may be followed by C major or C minor:

G   B   D   F—   B   D   F   A♭—D,   F,   A♭,   C.
First. Third. Fifth. Seventh. Third. Fifth. Seventh. Minor Fifth. Seventh. Minor Eleventh.
                                        ninth.   ninth.

(The ninth, if present, must be minor, as the major ninth cannot be used in a minor key.)

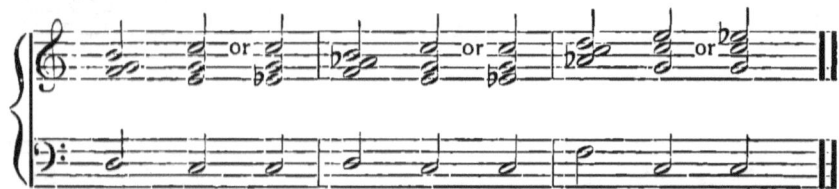

It will at once be seen that, by taking advantage of this fact, **Three Transitions** may be made from a given key by changing the major tonics to Minor, and three by changing the Minor tonics to major.

1. The tonic of the principal key is changed to Minor, and as C minor is the relative minor of E♭, the Transition is from C to E♭.
2. The same process in the related key of G takes us to B♭.
3. The same process in the related key of F takes us to A♭.

This means of making Transition may be combined with that first given. It would require volumes of examples to illustrate them. We give a few, leaving it to the pupil to invent others,— an easy task if the principles are kept in mind.

To analyze a Transition, always observe what relation each chord bears to the chord and key that precedes it, and to the chord and key that follows it.

1. Dominant harmony of G, fifth to eleventh, followed by G minor (2). This is then treated as being a third of $E\flat$, and is followed by dominant of $E\flat$. 3. Same process repeated in $E\flat$, but the minor chord (4), $B\flat$, is treated as subdominant of F minor, the parallel of F major.

In the next examples the supertonic harmonics of the three major keys of the group are followed by minor tonics.

Write corresponding modulations in all keys; also make the corresponding changes in the related minor keys.

A **Third** means of Transition is by Additions to common chords.

To a Major chord, the minor third below its root may be added; it then becomes fifth, seventh, major ninth, and eleventh of a dominant. This addition to the first and fourth chords will not give a transition, unless the ninth is minor (see former rule), but it will with the fifth.

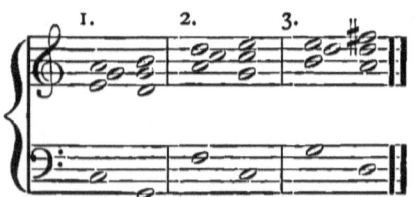

1. C, E, G, with A, the minor third below, added. If the E were changed to $E\flat$, the tonic of G minor might follow, giving a transition to $B\flat$.

2. Same remarks will apply.

3. G, B, D, becoming dominant eleventh of D major.

The augmented sixth over the root may be added to any major chord. This gives some startling Transitions. Like the supertonic harmony, a major or minor tonic may follow. (1 and 2), if followed by *minor* tonics, resolve within the group. (3), out of the group whether major or minor tonic be used after it.

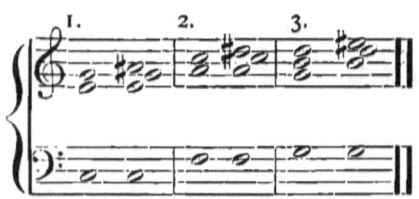

According to our rule the raised note must be the third. Therefore $F\sharp$ is the root of 1, and as $F\sharp$ is the supertonic of E, this is the augmented sixth of E. Root of second is B; of third, $C\sharp$.

HARMONY. 137

A minor third below the root may be added to a minor chord. It may be fifth, seventh, minor ninth, and eleventh of a dominant, or third, fifth, seventh, and major ninth of a dominant or supertonic.

1. *D, F, A*, with *B* added, treated as dominant eleventh of *A* major or minor.
2. Same, treated as dominant ninth of *C*.
3. Same, treated as supertonic ninth of *F*.
4 and 5. Are the remaining minor chords in *C*, with minor third below added.

These and the preceding examples with major chords should be all written out and resolved.

The addition of a minor third *above* a Minor chord has the same result as the addition of a minor third *below* a Major chord.

The next means of making Transition is by the **Chromatic Alteration** of chords; first, from major to minor, and the reverse; second, changing a group of four sounds into some other group of four sounds.

Thus the group *G, B, D, F* (first, third, fifth, seventh of dominant of supertonic) may be changed into third, fifth, seventh, ninth, by making *G* sharp.

Into fifth, seventh, ninth, eleventh by making *B* flat.

Into fifth, seventh, ninth, eleventh, or third, fifth, seventh, ninth by making *B* and *D* flat.

Into third, fifth, seventh, ninth by making *B, D,* and *F* flat.

Last, by flatting *D* it becomes an augmented sixth chord, *D♭, F, G,* and *B*.

Write out these changes and resolve them.

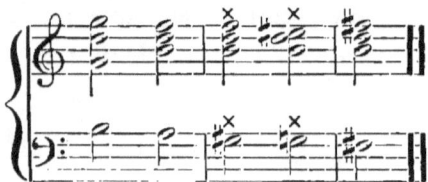

In the course of this change one or more of the sounds may be enharmonically changed.

The last means by which Transitions may be made is by **Enharmonic Change**.

First, advantage may be taken of the fact that the dominant seventh chord and augmented sixth chord sound alike, consequently the seventh may be changed to an augmented sixth, or the reverse.

This change is not always expressed in the writing.

1. Dominant of *F*, changed to augmented sixth of *E*.

1. Augmented sixth of *C*, changed to dominant of *D♭*.

At *a* the dominant of *C* is treated as the augmented sixth of *B*, the enharmonic change being implied.

At *b* the augmented sixth of *B* is changed back to the dominant of *C*. The change is implied here also, but it differs from the first case in that the chord is written according to its resolution, whereas in the first case it is not.

The chief source of enharmonic modulation is found in the diminished seventh chords.

These chords consist of four sounds separated from each other by three half-tones; thus, *B*, *D*, *F*, *A*♭.
                Third Fifth. Seventh. Ninth.

It will be found that, no matter in what order they are written, this will hold good; therefore, any one of the sounds may be in turn, the third, fifth, seventh, or ninth. Thus if *A*♭ be put at the bottom we get, *A*♭, *B*, *D*, *F*, and the *A*♭ being enharmonically *G*♯, the chord may be written *G*♯, *B*, *D*, *F*.

Therefore, as there are four notes in the chord, it may be written in four ways, and obtained from four roots, and resolved in four ways as a dominant, and four ways as a supertonic harmony.

Take the group *B*, *D*, *F*, *A*♭ and move every sound up a half-tone; we get *C*, *E*♭, *F*♯, *A*♮. Move these up a half-tone; we get *C*♯, *E*♮, *G*, *B*♭. Repeat the process, and we get the group with which we began. It will be seen that in the three groups all the sounds of the Chromatic Scale are included.

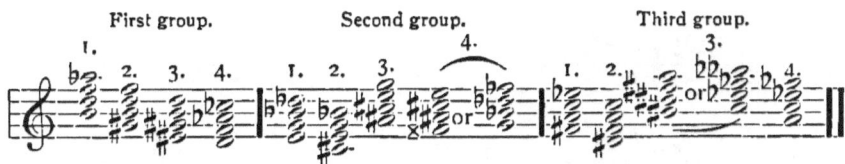

First group. 1. Written as if derived from *G*; therefore dominant of *C* major or minor, or supertonic of *F* major or minor.

2. As if derived from *E*; dominant of *A*, supertonic of *D*.

3. As if derived from *C*♯; dominant of *F*♯, supertonic of *B*.

4. As if derived from *B*♭; dominant of *E*♭, supertonic of *A*♭.

Second group. 1. As if derived from *C*; dominant of *F*, supertonic of *B*♭.

2. As if derived from *A*; dominant of *D*, supertonic of *G*.

3. As if derived from $F\sharp$; dominant of B, supertonic of E.

4. As if derived from $D\sharp$ or $E\flat$; dominant of $G\sharp$ or $A\flat$, supertonic of $C\sharp$ or $D\flat$.

Third group. 1. As if derived from D; dominant of G, supertonic of C.

2. As if derived from B; dominant of E, supertonic of A.

3. As if derived from $G\sharp$ or $A\flat$; dominant of $C\sharp$ or $D\flat$, supertonic of $F\sharp$ or $G\flat$.

4. As if derived from F; dominant of $B\flat$, supertonic of $E\flat$.

It will be seen that each group is found twice in every key; viz., in the dominant of the major, and in that of its relative minor. This being true in the scale of C, it follows that it must be so in every scale.

This fact makes it possible to change instantly from one key to another by means of this chord in two ways.

First way, take the group that contains the leading note of the key to which it is desired to go, and resolve it as a dominant harmony.

Second way, take the group containing the keynote of the key to which it is desired to go, and resolve it as a supertonic harmony.

It is a good practice, unfortunately not so much observed as it ought to be, to write the diminished seventh chord, when used for Transition, as it would be in the key in which it is resolved.

1. C to $F\sharp$ by dominant. 2. C to $F\sharp$ by supertonic. 3. C to $A\flat$, dominant. 4. C to $D\flat$, supertonic. 5. C to $B\flat$, dominant. 6. C to $G\flat$, supertonic. Observe that in each case the diminished seventh group is not written as it would be in C, but as it would be in the key that is to follow it.

One great advantage of writing it this way is, that it simplifies the reading, because a musician always reads the *harmony* as well as the *notes*, and is much more likely to trip over a miswritten passage than a difficult one.

The only way to master this protean chord is to write, or better still, play on the piano all the changes indicated by the foregoing remarks.

The diminished seventh may be changed into a group of first, third, fifth, and seventh in two ways. First, since any one of the notes may be considered as the ninth by lowering it half a tone, the note to which it is lowered becomes the root.

1. $D\flat$, lowered diatonically to C.
2. B lowered diatonically to A; $D\flat$, enharmonically changed to $C\sharp$.
3. G, lowered chromatically to $G\flat$; E, enharmonically changed to $F\flat$.
4. E, lowered chromatically to $E\flat$.

Second way, by retaining one note and moving the rest up a half-tone, the note retained becomes the root.

In both these cases the note that becomes the seventh may be enharmonically changed into an augmented sixth.

Last of all, the rules given in Chapter XVI. may be applied to this chord, which may be written in any of its four ways, as may best suit the succession desired.

Transitions are often effected by means of **Harmonic Sequences**.

The Harmonic Sequence consists of a dominant, or supertonic, or augmented sixth harmony followed by its resolution, repeated at regular intervals ascending or descending.

The varieties that may be made are infinite, but the following examples will give a clear idea of the operation.

1. Dominant and tonic; each a whole-tone below the last. The succession of dominant seventh will explain this passage.

2. Dominant and tonic; each a half-tone lower than the last. Each common chord bears the relation of tonic to the dominant that precedes it, and of lowered supertonic to the one that follows it.

3. Dominant and tonic; the minor ninth added; the *roots* ascend by fourths, each root a whole-tone above the preceding.

4. Is a reversal of 3. The *roots* descend by fourths, each root a whole-tone below the preceding.

All these sequences may be inverted or rearranged in any way.

A Sequence may take in three, four, or even more chords, as in the following examples.

1. Tonic, augmented sixth, dominant; ascends by whole-tones.

2. Tonic and dominant; each root has first a tonic, then a dominant harmony.

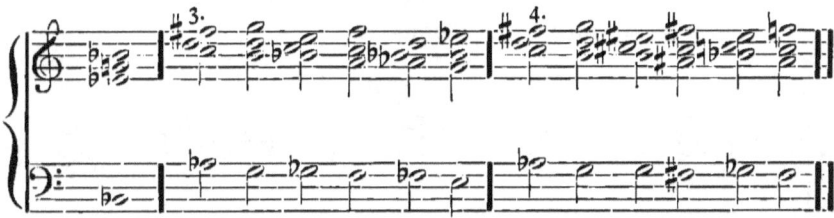

1. Supertonic harmony; tonic, dominant; descending by whole-tones.

2. The same, with supertonic harmony changed to augmented sixth.

3. Augmented sixth and dominant, descending by whole-tones; i. e., the roots.

4. Same, descending by half-tones; i. e., the roots.

Of course the sequence may be stopped at any point, when the key is reached to which it is wished to make a transition.

Sequences may be made by means of the second and third progressions of the dominant, also with dominant eleventh.

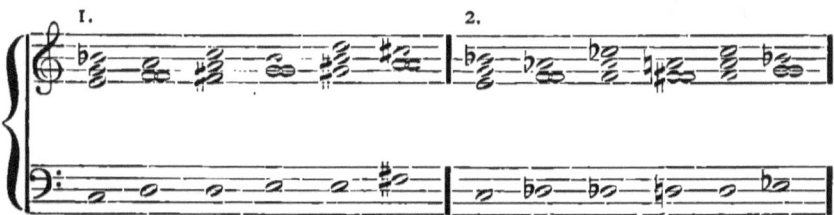

1. A sequence of second progressions; each dominant resolved as in a major key.
2. Same; the dominants resolved as in a minor key.
3. Sequence of third progressions.

1. Sequence with eleventh chords.
2. Same, showing the sudden transition that may be made by substituting *A* major for *A* minor.

The pupil should write and play these sequences in all the keys repeatedly, and should invent new ones, make inversions of them, and arrange the chords in different ways.

If the plan of instruction mapped out in this book has been carefully followed, and each step mastered before proceeding to the next, above all, if the **Relationship** of **Keys** making up the **"Group"** is well understood, the pupil will have a knowledge and command of the resources of harmony that will amply repay the time and labor spent in acquiring them.

SUPPLEMENT

Tempered Scale.

There is among musicians such a vague notion as to what is meant by the tempered scale, that it has been thought well to add a few explanatory words, avoiding all minute details as much as possible.

To make all our chords in perfect tune it would be necessary to divide the octave into so many parts that the result would be an unmanageable mass of sounds; but it was discovered that by dividing the octave as nearly as possible into twelve equal parts, a series of sounds was obtained, which while not corresponding exactly with the true series, was yet so near that every sound in the series might be the root, third, fifth, seventh, etc., in some chord, so nearly in tune that the ear was satisfied.

The gain to music was not alone in the simplification of the scale, but, what was of far greater importance, the power of passing at will from any key to any other, by taking advantage of the sounds they hold in common.

On this modern music is founded. It is hardly too much to say that modern music dates from the publication of the "Well Tempered Clavier."

Practically the "tempering" of the scale is secured by a very simple means; viz., by tuning every fifth slightly flat. This secures the twelvefold division of the octave.

The ratio between the vibrations, per second, of a given note and its octave is 1 to 2; that is, the octave vibrates twice as fast. The ratio between the vibrations, per second, of a given note and its fifth is 2 to 3; that is, the fifth vibrates one-half faster than the root.

Now suppose we begin with *C*, and tune in fifths and octaves as in the following diagram.

It will be seen that by tuning *up* twelve fifths and *down* six octaves, the octave of the first note is reached.

Now, if we allow 144 vibrations to the starting note, the octave must have 288; but the *C* reached by the tuning given above will have about 290, so that it is too sharp, about the one-eighth of a tone.

Tempering is dividing this small interval, called the comma of Pythagoras from its reputed discoverer, as equally as possible among the twelve fifths. The result is that the octave is the only interval in our system that is perfectly in tune.

Below will be found the first six of the above sounds, with their vibration numbers attached. It is an easy arithmetical problem to find the rest. To find the fifth of a given sound, add half the number to itself; thus, *C*, 144; *G*, 216, because the half of 144 is 72, and 72 and 144 are 216. When the octave *below* is to be found, divide the number by 2.

It is not necessary here to go any deeper into this subject. The student who wishes to become thoroughly acquainted with it will find it exhaustively treated in many works on acoustics, especially in Helmholtz, Tyndal, Blaserna, etc. There is also an excellent treatise in "Grove's Dictionary," under the title Temperament.

The regret is often expressed that musicians do not adopt a more perfect scale, but it should not be forgotten that custom rules in this as in many other things. From our earliest infancy we are habituated to the tempered scale.

It is the scale that has given us all the greatest music we possess; it satisfied the musical instincts of Bach, Haydn, Mozart, Beethoven, Mendelssohn, and countless others among the greatest composers.

Music means something more than mere sweet sound. To one who feels this meaning, no possible exactness of intonation would add to it in, say, the slow movement of the Sonata Pathétique (I choose an illustration from piano music because the chief scorn of the purists is directed against the piano), while on the other hand it would quite destroy the unexpected modulation from $A\flat$ to E, and back again.

There is but one way in which a change in our scale may be introduced: some great composer must arise who will show us that its possibilities for expression far surpass those of the tempered scale.

FIGURED BASS.

Called also Erroneously Thorough Bass, (Italian) Basso Continuo, (German) General Bass.

Figured bass was devised as a sort of musical shorthand, by means of which the chord each bass note was to bear was represented by figures placed under or over the bass. Its use dates from about the year 1600. It was intended to serve as a guide to the accompanist, to whose discretion it was left to arrange the harmony as he pleased. It may easily be guessed that accompaniment did not have the importance in the estimation of the old composers that it has in their modern successors.

By one of those strange chances that so often happen, figured bass has assumed a position never contemplated by its inventors, through its adoption as the means of teaching harmony. Its original purpose has long been disused, although conservatism still demands "playing from figured bass" as one of the exercises for candidates for degrees at some universities.

It may be easily understood that it is quite possible for any one to write over a given series of notes the intervals indicated by the figures, without having the least conception of the reasons for the combinations or for their successions. Just as one may learn the Greek alphabet so as to pronounce with facility the Greek language, yet without knowing the meaning of a single word.

The principles upon which the system of figured bass is constructed are easily understood, and to anyone who has mastered the system of harmony taught in this book, they offer no difficulties.

The simple combinations and successions of the older writers may be represented with comparatively little complexity, but the most ardent advocates of figured bass admit that the amount of complication made necessary in the figuring by the complexity of modern music, is such that its unravelment becomes a veritable enigma.

The rules upon which the system is based are as follows (the figures indicate the intervals over the bass):

When a note is without figures it bears the common chord.

1. But it is sometimes necessary, as for example, when a given note is to bear two or more chords, to indicate the common chord by a 3, or 5, or $\frac{5}{3}$, or $\frac{8}{5}$, etc. (As a general thing, the 3 is sufficient.)

2. The position of the chord is left entirely to the discretion, or the reverse, of the student.

The figures must be written with the largest unit at the top, without regard to the member of the chord that may occupy this position; thus,

$\frac{7}{5}$ may be
3

When this arrangement is departed from, it means that the intervals must be arranged in the way indicated by the figures; thus,

The first inversion of a common chord is figured ⁶₃, or 6 only; the rule being that where 6 is used 3 is understood to accompany it (1). The second inversion is figured ⁶₄ (2).

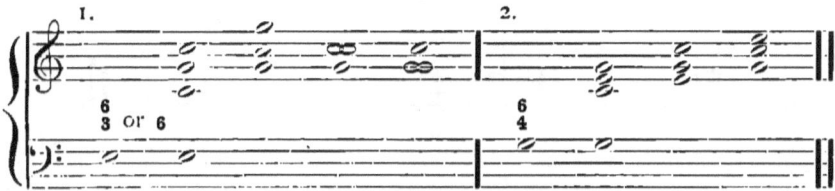

The figure 7 (for ⁷₅₃) indicates any of the following groups:

Dominant or supertonic, first to seventh, third to ninth, or fifth to eleventh, or a passing seventh, or a suspended seventh (1).

The first inversion of ⁷₅₃ is figured ⁶₅, a 3 being understood (1); the second inversion of ⁷₅₃ is figured ⁴₃, a 6 being understood (2); the third inversion of ⁷₅₃ is figured ⁴₂, a 6 being understood (3).

(As in the former case it applies to any four note group.)

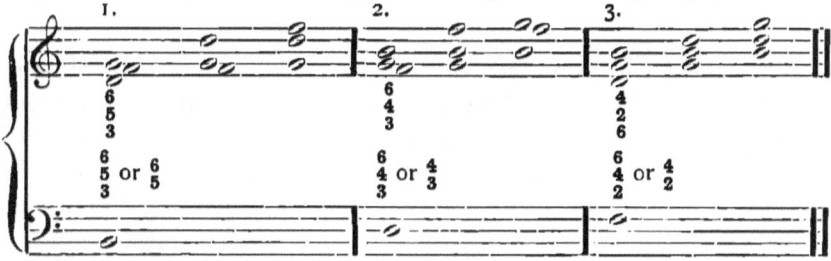

Accidentals are indicated as follows:

When sharp, flat, or natural is placed over a note *not* followed by a figure, it always refers to the third-over the bass (1). When sharp, flat, or natural is followed by a figure, it affects the member of the chord for which that figure stands (2).

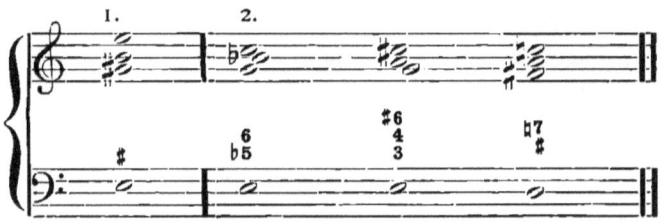

There are two exceptions, viz., the augmented sixth is indicated by a six with a line through it, thus, ⑥; the augmented fourth is indicated in the same way, ⚡.

When a note is common to two or more chords in succession, its repetition is indicated by means of short horizontal lines (1).

A long line placed after the figures, over the first note of a running or arpeggioed bass, means that the chord is to be held until the end of the line (2).

When there are several sets of figures over a single note, care must be taken to get the value of the notes in which the chords are written correctly. When there are two or four sets of figures over a note, there is no difficulty; but when there are three or any other odd number, it is not so easy to tell just how the values are to be dis-

SUPPLEMENT.

tributed. This is indicated in some degree by the position of the figures in the measure; thus,

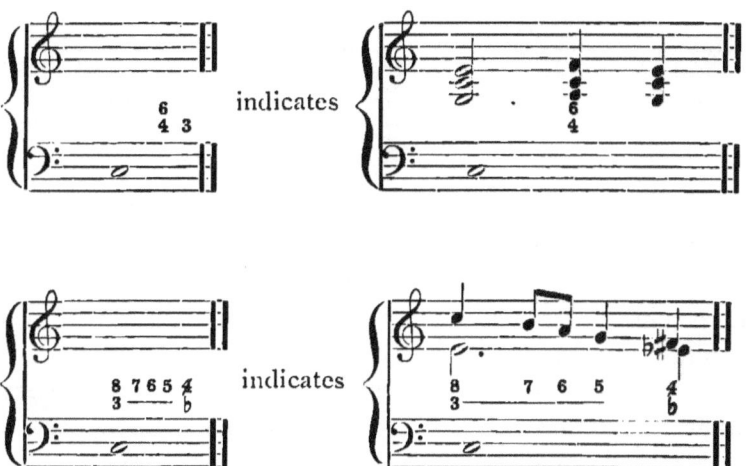

Various attempts have been made to improve on this system of figured bass by the use of additional signs, but the increase in the number of signs only increases the complexity.

One plan largely adopted, is to indicate the degree of the scale that is the root of the chord by means of Roman numerals under the chords.

Thus, $\genfrac{}{}{0pt}{}{\frac{4}{3}}{V}$ signifies that the chord is an inversion of the chord whose root is the fifth of the scale.

Another plan that has never become general uses the letters of the alphabet to indicate the member of the chord that is used as a bass; thus,

A signifies that the root is at the bass.
B signifies that the third is at the bass.
C signifies that the fifth is at the bass.
D signifies that the seventh is at the bass.
E signifies that the ninth is at the bass.
F signifies that the eleventh is at the bass.
G signifies that the thirteenth is at the bass.

Enough has been written to give the student a thorough understanding of the meaning of Figured Bass. Should any one wish to pursue the subject farther there are innumerable text-books based on this system that may be consulted.

That good musicians may be trained by this system countless numbers attest. We only claim for the system set forth here, that it reaches the same results by a shorter and pleasanter route.

www.ingramcontent.com/pod-product-compliance
Lightning Source LLC
Chambersburg PA
CBHW020309170426
43202CB00008B/551